MW00585620

Motherhood

Motherhood

A Confession

NATALIE CARNES

STANFORD UNIVERSITY PRESS
Stanford, California

STANFORD UNIVERSITY PRESS
Stanford, California

© 2020 by the Board of Trustees of the Leland Stanford Junior University.
All rights reserved.

No part of this book may be reproduced or transmitted in any form or by any means, electronic or mechanical, including photocopying and recording, or in any information storage or retrieval system without the prior written permission of Stanford University Press.

Printed in the United States of America on acid-free, archival-quality paper

LIBRARY OF CONGRESS CATALOGING-IN-PUBLICATION DATA
Names: Carnes, Natalie, author.
Title: Motherhood : a confession / Natalie Carnes.
Description: Stanford, California : Stanford University Press, 2020. |
    Includes bibliographical references.
Identifiers: LCCN 2019037471 (print) | LCCN 2019037472 (ebook) |
    ISBN 9781503608313 (cloth) | ISBN 9781503612310 (epub)
Subjects: LCSH: Motherhood—Religious aspects—Christianity.
Classification: LCC BV4529.18 .C376 2020 (print) | LCC BV4529.18 (ebook) |
    DDC 248.8/431—dc23
LC record available at https://lccn.loc.gov/2019037471
LC ebook record available at https://lccn.loc.gov/2019037472

Cover design: David Drummond

Text design: Kevin Barrett Kane

This book is typeset in Adobe Caslon Pro, designed by Carol Twombly in 1990, based on William Caslon's specimen pages printed between 1734–1770

For Chora, Edith, and Simone

CONTENTS

Reborn

S ome women long for motherhood. Yearning for a child, they receive news of their pregnancy with elation. It is to them glad tidings of great joy. I was untouched by that desire when I began to suspect, with dim horror, that I might be pregnant. Alone in our bathroom, I confirmed my suspicion, and wept. For several days, my bewildered husband consoled me before asking gently, tentatively, when I might be ready to celebrate our news. Not yet.

How could I celebrate? I had no room for a child. I was not halfway through my doctoral program. I was negotiating a new marriage. I had no real income. What I had were anxieties and ambitions so bloated they seemed to crowd out any space for new life. How could I teach my first classes, finish my degree, and land an academic job with a baby? Somewhere I had latched on to the notion that people raise children after their own journey of development reached some kind of conclusion, or at least a plateau, and I felt far from any arrival. Even so, pregnancy was upon me, falling invisibly and heavily on my body.

Nausea deflated my angst and sustained me. For months, I lived in a fog of sickness. When it lifted, I saw that a powerful love for my daughter had already taken shape. That love and nausea together carried me to the final hours of my pregnancy, when I found myself huddled in a tub, racked by contractions. Everything in those moments was stripped away—my labor strategies, my contraction mantras, my images, my plans, my clothes. The pain and urgency of labor left me exposed. Perhaps for the only time since my childhood, I was naked and unashamed. There was a final burst of pain and effort, and my daughter arrived.

As clearly as I remember my daughter's birth, I can summon no memory, however faint or blurred, of my own. But who can? As a conscious memory, my birth is lost to me, even though it is my very beginning, even as it stays somewhere in my bodily memory, shaping my relation to the world. My infancy is long dead, Augustine writes, and yet I am alive.

The loss and ongoing presence of our births is mirrored in the narrative of Jesus in the Gospel of John. There is no infancy narrative in that gospel, no angelic announcement of birth, no donkey-riding Mary great with child, no magi seeking the babe, no boy growing in wisdom and stature. John's book opens with Word and Light present in the beginning. When Jesus appears, he is an adult; when his mother enters the stage, she provokes his first miracle and signals that his ministry is underway. There is no story of physical birth—but neither is birth absent from the gospel. As our own births mark us in mysterious and implicit ways, so birth remains both unnarrated in the Gospel of John and also ever-present, pervading it in metaphors and images.

The first mention of birth in John's Gospel comes from Jesus's conversation with Nicodemus. *Truly, truly, I say to you, no one can see the kingdom of God unless she is born again.* Today, rebirth is so common a way of naming conversion that it has become stale and obvious. But to Nicodemus, Jesus's words are nonsense. *How can anyone be born when he is old? Shall I crawl back into my mother's womb?* Patiently, Jesus distinguishes earthly from heavenly and physical from spiritual. He redirects Nicodemus to a different womb, implying a different parent, and arriving, finally, at a second subtle meditation on parenthood, in which God lovingly sends God's only-begotten Son to give life to the world.

Bookending Jesus's conversation with Nicodemus are two encounters with John the Baptist, who baptizes Jesus prior to the conversation and testifies about him after. In the episode following his reunion with John, Jesus, too, begins baptizing—or at least his disciples do. Language of birth abounds in these first few chapters: the rebirth metaphors for conversion, the descriptions of Jesus as the only-begotten Son of God, the baptisms of and by Jesus. Images of wombs and mothers and waters of parturition seep into the book, enlivening descriptions of conversion and new life. Birth, as metaphor and image, is everywhere. The early church dramatized the birth imagery of baptism by requiring the baptized to enter the waters naked, dipping their entire body into a font shaped like a womb or a coffin, as the baptized died to their old life and were reborn in the womb of God, the new mother of their new childhood.

Yet we don't always see how motherhood, infancy, and children disclose what it means to be human in relation to the divine. For centuries, Christian texts exploring humanness have come from men reflecting on their own flesh. Generation after generation of Christians has spoken of God with masculine pronouns and titles that have ossified into literal referents. Women and children have remained largely absent from talk of divinity and humanity. But what if their lives were taken as significant sites for theological work? What if their bodies were seen as revelatory of human life as it encounters and fails to encounter divine presence? What if the most influential reflection on humanity in the Western world centered not on the struggles of a man's body but on those of a woman's or a child's? How might a woman's or child's *Confessions* go?

I don't remember the first time I encountered Augustine's *Confessions*, but I remember the first time its pathos sank into my imagination. I was studying for my master's degree in theology, and Augustine's story of desire—its betrayals and its transformations—gripped me. In the midst of a tumultuous breakup, I was struck by one episode in particular: the conclusion of Augustine's faithful relationship with his common-law wife of over ten years, whose social status deemed her unfit to be his legitimate wife. Augustine describes this woman as ripped from his side, leaving his heart wounded, torn, and trailing blood. She vows ongoing, separated faithfulness to him as she leaves both Augustine and their son, named Adeodatus or "gift of God," to return to Africa. We know what happened to Augustine. What happened to this woman, whom he loved so ardently for a time? She never appears again in the story. How would she have narrated their relationship and its end? Was her heart restless? Did it find rest?

Twice in the next few years I taught the *Confessions* as a teaching assistant. On the second occasion, I guest-lectured on it for a course on happiness and the life of virtue. I was pregnant for the first time and entering into a new life of desire, one that the *Confessions* spoke to only obliquely. Though the *Confessions* still captivated me; though it has continued since then to nourish me as a teacher, reader, and seeker; though I teach it even now every semester, I found and continue to find its characterizations of parenthood and childhood unsatisfying. The *Confessions* does not offer the wealth of insight about life with children one might expect from so thoughtful a book, despite the presence of Augustine's own mother, Monica, his son, Adeodatus, and the scenes of his own infancy. Augustine renders his own life and motivations textured, compelling, and complex, but depictions of his mother's, his son's, and his childhood self's are flat and sparse.

Rather than attempt the imaginative feat of resurrecting the inner lives of Monica, Adeodatus, or Augustine's partner, I stay much closer to home—my home—by reflecting on the conversions and desires in my own life with small children. I bring alongside Augustine's great text another narrative of what it means to be human, for childhood and parenthood have dramas not identical to those of the single male. Augustine struggles over the course of the *Confessions* for his scattered self to be gathered, his divided will to become whole. Yet the central drama of parenthood is not of two wills becoming one; it is of one will becoming two, as the parent helps bring the child's will into fullness.

In some ways, the book I have written echoes the *Confessions*. I have followed Augustine in writing thirteen chapters, and each of my chapters centers on a theme found in his book. Like him, I cast my narrative in the second person. However, where Augustine addresses God, I address my daughter for the first nine chapters before turning directly to God in the final four, a turning that parallels Augustine's shift from narrating a story to entering a more purely reflective mode, a reflection upon reflection. I preserve Augustine's two levels of reflection while also exploring what it means to address God through a creature, how the "you" of my daughter turns toward and away from the You of God. While the reader unacquainted with Augustine will find she can enter these reflections as well as the expert, the reader familiar with the *Confessions* will notice critiques, appreciations, and subtle shifts that add up to a distinct picture of human life with God. Augustine's glittering vices become potential virtues in the making, his cup that is half empty of goodness becomes half filled with it. Life is riven with treachery and violence, but there can be less worry about the multiplicity of desire and can be instead more hopefulness about desires that fall short of the divine. It is a story of God meeting us in strange places as humans try, fail, and learn to help one another become more human. But now I am ahead of myself. I was only at birth, at the words of Jesus so banal to us and so confounding to Nicodemus. *Truly, truly, I say to you, no one can see the kingdom of God unless she is born again.*

It is night, shortly after the birth. Converted, I turn my attention to you in a new way. We are both damp from our births, wrapped in blankets, exhilarated and exhausted from our separation and new togetherness. We have lost the dependable relationship of care we knew for nine months. My body no longer tends to you as one of its own organs. I learn to minister to you as one body loving another. We try, for the first time, to suckle. By midnight you have taken some milk, and we both fall asleep. In a few hours, our new world will dawn. We awake in the morning to new life.

Motherhood

PART I

To My Daughter

CHAPTER 1

Idolatry

*How shall I call upon my God, my God and Lord? Surely
when I call on him, I am calling on him to come into me.
But what place is there in me where my God can enter
me? "God made heaven and earth." Where may he come
to me? Lord my God, is there any room in me which can
contain you?*

In the beginning, you were my secret. I looked to all the world
the same. I seemed, for a *very* short time, the same to myself.
For those first few days, I put my entire faith in your existence
in a thin blue line on a white stick. You were a small piece of my
body, hidden in my body. You were my secret—secret, in many
ways, even to me.

I recently heard a planetary scientist on the radio speaking
about why we might want to orbit a far-off rock like Jupiter,
and she said, "I think we all want to know where we came from,
how our solar system got to be the way it is." It is a powerful
urge, to understand who we are by tracing our origins. Someday you will ask me about your own roots, and I will tell you
that you began as a secret, mine and your father's. And in some

ways, you will always be a secret, in the way a mystery is a type of secret. I thought as a parent I would feel your infant presence as an extension of my own and that I would relate to you as my own body—or at least as flesh and blood I myself had produced, shaped, and molded. But my overwhelming sense is how mysterious and separate you are. Where do your desires come from? What causes you to kick your legs, grunt, and whoop? What do you see as you gaze, lover-like, into my eyes for minutes on end? What gives you *this kind* of vitality?

The source of your you-ness will always be a secret, but in the beginning, the secret was different. Even the fact that there was a you was a secret, and your father and I kept it. Or we tried to. Somehow friends and family sensed your presence. Perhaps I didn't seem so unchanged as I thought. Even before you were visible, you must have been transforming me, projecting by way of me your presence into the world.

When you were within me, the people who knew you best were the midwives. They would tell me about you, sending me reports on your life, as ones who have traveled to distant planets and returned with alien intelligence. Early in my pregnancy, when your existence was no longer a secret but still fresh news, the midwives said, "The baby is the size of a grape, and needs plenty of calcium. Be sure to eat so many grams of it because"—they said this part with too much cheer—"your body will take calcium from your bones to give it to your baby."

I began to see not just the mystery of your existence, but my own strangeness in our new life together. My body still looked the same, like it was just going about its primary business of keeping itself alive—while my bones were hollowing themselves to help you grow? Bizarre and beautiful thought. Who is this calcium-consumer inside me? And who is this bone-sacrificer I have become? In this new world of our existence together, I make you from my very body, giving to you despite the cost to me. It is unlike anything I have ever done. In that conversation about calcium, I realized that I was playing a role no sane person claims with a straight face and no Christian accepts without fear and trembling. I was—as my body swelled and I lumbered ungracefully around the house—like a god to you.

Or, more modestly, I was your first image of divinity. My body was your cosmos, the source that filled your needs and sustained your life. From your dark and watery perspective, I was your creator. In the beginning, I gave you a universe that was formless and void, and darkness covered your face. You knew me as a voice, a breath that vibrated over the waters of my womb. In the beginning, we were as creator and creature, playing out the story of your genesis.

In your need of me, you were also God to me. You were the God who comes to us in Christ needing food, drink, and shelter, the Christ who comes as a stranger, patient, and prisoner. Whatever is done for the least of these, Jesus preaches in the gospel of Matthew, is done unto Christ. Jesus in this passage imagines himself both as the gloriously returning Lord and the Lord hidden in the least of these. And who was less than you in my womb? You were the utterly vulnerable one, the one whose life depended hourly on my hospitality. Little one, least of these, you were Christ to me.

But the story is more layered still. As you were Christ to me, so I was Christ to you. I was the Christ who first found humanity exposed and sheltered us with the church, who saw us hungry and gave us the food of the Eucharist, who knew us as strangers and then made us friends. I was the Christ whom Christ calls us to imitate, the Christ whose ministry to the least of these founds our own. I was Christ who, in my bone-sacrifice of calcium, lays down her life for her friends.

I was only Christ in a shadowy way, of course. I did not give the church, the Eucharist, or atonement. I gave my body, blood, and bones, though not because I chose this sacrifice. Still, my gift was a faint echo, a sign, of Christ's gifts. Through pregnancy, my body became charitable, my life given for the sake of another. You were teaching me in my very bones the little way of love. Is it any wonder that Saint Thérèse of Lisieux—she who wrote of the little way of love and aspired to small sacrifices of love as simple and ordinary as life itself—took as her name for religious life Thérèse of the Child Jesus? With her name, she links childhood with this little way of love. The maternal body reiterates that connection as it nurtures a child through little sacrifices as ordinary as life itself.

The body's sacrifices may be small and ordinary, but they can nevertheless be costly. I keep thinking about calcium. I think about my grandmother and her multiple falls, which turned into multiple breaks because she suffered from osteoporosis late in life, precipitated by having born and birthed four children. I think of my mother, who herself bore three children, watching her mother's decline and taking up weight-bearing exercises and calcium chews. We do not choose to send calcium from our bones or to make these other sacrifices of care. Our bodies simply do these things, caring for the vulnerable one within as if charity were the grain of the universe, as if we were already a charitable people.

You made charity natural to me. Without my choosing, you made me more merciful because you came to me like Christ. You came as Christ to me, not because you were divine or sinless but because like Christ, you came to me as a stranger in need, offering grace. The gift of your needy presence taught me to receive you, my own vulnerable stranger, so that by that practice of hospitality, I might learn to receive Christ. With you pressing against the walls of my belly, finding no room to grow, I learned to make space for God. And so through you, my small creation, I found and became more like my uncontainable Creator. In your dependent existence, God came to me in a new way.

One day, when I was about twenty weeks pregnant, I heard on the news that you womb-dwellers give your mothers fetal cells. When stories about pregnancy or children came on the radio, I paused what I was doing and turned up the volume. That day, I learned about fetal cells that cross the placenta into the woman's body, where they stay for years after her pregnancy. Though they are found in many different tissues in the mother's body, they seem particularly drawn to sites of injury. They have been found making collagen in C-section scars, and they may act as guards against cancer cells. In an experiment on mice, fetal cells responded to a stroke in the mother by repairing damaged blood vessels. One study reports that fetal cells "selectively home to injured maternal hearts." Your baby cells, which you gave me without any choice or even awareness, help tend the wounds in my body and repair any brokenness in my heart. What could be a better image of the divine than giving one's body to bind broken hearts? As God came to humanity in Christ like a healer tending the sick, so you entered into my bloodstream, finding any injuries to restore me to wholeness. You in your fetal cells practiced merciful care even before you knew what mercy was. I remember looking down at my growing belly and my swollen ankles and wondering about those cells of yours swimming through my veins, schooling me into the way of mercy.

There is something else you have in common with Christ. Christ, too, came into the world by a womb. The God who made heaven and earth came as one of the least of these, harbored in the body of the woman who became God's mother. There is no room which can contain God, but God entered the uterus, the smallest room anyone ever inhabits. Mary's hospitable yes drew

the uncontainable God into the world, and her swollen belly became the first glimpse of Christ, the human-God.

In a way, Mary's God-imaging body was anticipated by the
ancient goddess statues that imagine the divine as covered with
breasts. I recently showed my class a slide of one of these remark-
able, many-breasted statues, named Artemis of Ephesus. Breasts
fill her entire torso. Her headpiece and dress are alive with animals. She is meant to be a life-giver, sharing her fecundity with the
world. Artemis, like other breasted gods, attempts to give form to
the immensity of creating and sustaining life. She is imposing and
dynamic, her surfaces crawling with life. Sometimes Christians
have been anxious about such statues, condemning them as idols
and emphasizing their unlikeness to the God of Abraham, Isaac,
Jacob, and Jesus Christ—and no doubt the statues can and have
functioned as idols. But can I also see these statues as attempts at
imagining and praising God? Receiving the statues in this spirit,
I see them searching for a creaturely analogy for a creator divinity,
and finding it in a woman who gives life to another through her
body. Here is one way to praise your God, they might say, to praise
God as the Great Mother who suckles all creation to life.

The Christian God did not settle for giving us creaturely anal-
ogies for the divine. In the central moment of the Christian story,
God came as a creature. In Christ, God came, not as a fertile
woman, graced with a life-giving body, but as a babe, like you, who
required a mother's body. The God who was like us in all ways
except sin shared our most vulnerable state. It is a central mystery
of Christianity that God in the newborn Christ is at once both
helpless and all-powerful. God the mother of all creation came
as the neediest creature within it, a baby. Breathtaking as she is,
Artemis falls short both of this power and this vulnerability.

Like the Christ-babe, like all babies, you eventually left the
womb. No longer swimming in my body, you have become a land

Idolatry

creature, like me and separate from me. When you were in my womb, my body bore the burden of care without waiting for or requiring my consent. Only in rather minimal ways did I willingly participate: avoiding scotch, eating well, submitting to medical care. My body provided all your material needs. In birth, my body is relieved of some of its burdens, and I learn new ways of nurturing your life. It is a shift for you, no doubt. It is also a huge shift for me. Margaret Mead once wrote, "The mother who must learn that the infant who was but an hour ago a part of her own body is now a different individual, with its own hungers and its own needs, and that if she listens to her own body to interpret the child, the child will die, is schooled in an irreplaceable school." I am being schooled in the irreplaceable school of your separateness. My hunger is no longer your hunger. I learn to tend to you—to know your cries, your expressions, your squirms. Through our separateness, I learn attunement to you.

As I attune to your needs, I discover that you are initially a slow nurser. The first few days, even weeks, you are sleepy, not yet awake to your own desires. In the womb, everything you needed arrived before you could want it, and you seem in the period after birth to expect that pattern to continue. You have not learned, or felt compelled, to reach for what you need. I feel my swollenness and try to coax you to take some milk. You eventually agree and leisurely take in some nourishment. But soon your desires seem boundless. Certainly they are not bounded by hunger. You nurse for many reasons—because you are scared or tired or because you want to be close to me. You nurse for reassurance and pleasure and comfort. One day you nurse every hour.

Did God in infancy nurse only when hungry and thirsty? Or did God nurse also when sleepy, fearful, or wanting Mary? How did God as a baby feel when Mary held the six-months-older child of her kinswoman Elizabeth? Did young Jesus tolerate

Mary's affections toward John the Baptist, or did he protest when asked to share her? What if Mary were watching Elizabeth's son, and he cried for milk? Would she have nursed baby John? Would Jesus have happily shared his milk with his cousin? Or would he, as Augustine describes his infant self, have grown pale watching another take his mother's milk?

What is a mother to make of her baby's singular desire for milk? Augustine observed the desire uneasily in his son, projecting backward into his own life as an infant and outward to all humanity. "Who reminds me of the sins of my infancy?" he asks. "Was it wrong that in tears I greedily opened my mouth wide to suck the breasts?" This is not a difficult question for Augustine—it seems obvious to him that the greed was wrong. Today, Augustine's judgment seems strange. We lightly excuse, or even sentimentalize, a child's insistent desire for milk and disinclination to share it. It is a phase to us, and it will pass. But to Augustine, the phase passes into a more sinister kind of greed, for it's evidence of humanity's conception in iniquity.

Is your single-minded nursing a sign of your iniquity? After your first sleepy days, your desire for milk grows to a voracious appetite. A few months after you are born, my day is busy. I am revising an article coming due, preparing for the next day's class, and grading a stack of papers. But the babysitter keeps knocking on the door, apologetically bringing you to me. Is it possible you are hungry again? Nursing, I look down at you. You smile mischievously, somehow remaining latched on the breast as you do. Keeping my gaze with your big, impish eyes, you give a happy grunt. What kind of greed could this be?

Sarah Hrdy tells me it's about your survival. An evolutionary biologist, Hrdy casts the story of mothers nursing babies in a much larger arc, dating to the beginnings of maternal lactation 220 million years ago. Babies at that time began to be born especially vulnerable. The mother who was not attuned to her infant's condition would lose the baby to starvation, dehydration, or exposure, and so natural selection favored babies and mothers sensitive to one another's signals and bodies. Lactation requires a high level of attunement to the baby's appearances, smells, and sounds. Lactation also helps to create this attunement. The first mission of a mammal baby, Hrdy writes, is "stimulating and conditioning its mother making sure that she becomes addicted to nursing" and so also more attuned to the baby's signals. Now after millennia of lactation, mammal mothers are highly attuned to their babies. Hrdy thinks of a mother dog who keeps returning to her litter, "nosing each pup, alert to distress, sensing their needs, suckling babies, keeping them warm." She likens the mother dog to a human mother, who returns to her baby every fifteen minutes to make sure he is breathing.

I think of your father as I read about the mother dog. He was constantly anxious about your breath those first few nights. I slept exhausted between nursing sessions, oblivious to his worry. Or maybe—perhaps this is what Hrdy might rejoin—I slept soundly because I trusted he was anxiously checking on you. For though he cannot lactate in the way a woman can, your father, too, is part of an animal group that has survived by the attunements of lactation. And we are all of us from a particular species that has survived by cooperative breeding and investment in one another's well-being. Hrdy points out that human mothers need help given the long time it takes for you children to grow and the many needs you have during your path to maturity. Lactation is what makes us the committed mothers that, as mammals, we are and gives rise to conditions in which we become the kind of species that has allomothers—"other mothers"—like fathers, grandparents, babysitters, and older siblings.

In our own species, the attunements born of lactation are part of what protects babies from abandonment. Nursing apparently stimulates hormonal and neurological responses in the mother that, along with other sensory cues, generates a strong attachment. Once mother and child have suckled, the mother has bonded to the infant, her desire for it surpassing all other considerations. So I think about you and your occasionally constant nursing and how this practice solidifies the infant-mother bond that ensures your survival—as if you are desiring me to desire you. It is such a complex desire, your desire to nurse. Can one narrate it as sin without slipping into nonsense?

Even Augustine has softer moments when he recounts his infancy. At the end of his meditations on sin in babyhood, Augustine claims that he feels no responsibility for the actions of his infancy. Is that a recognition that his "greedy nursing" is something other than human sin—or that it is, at the very least, a sin incomparable with adult sin? Sections earlier, he even has a positive account of nursing. What he calls "the consolations of human milk" welcome Augustine into life. The consolation was most directly from his mother or nurses, but ultimately from God, who filled their breasts and seeded the natural order with gifts. "For the good which came to me from them was a good for them; yet it was not from them but through them." The milk was God's gift to baby Augustine, God's gift to you, God's gift to baby God, to welcome the infant into the world. Augustine learned this later in life when God called out to him through other gifts. The gifts of creation taught him what gifts were and how to receive them as such.

I find these Augustinian insights helpful for thinking about you and your desire. Your desire for milk is excessive—and in that excessiveness, the desire points beyond itself. It suggests a desire that has not yet found its end. Mingled with hunger, thirst, and the need for human comfort is a desire that will not be satisfied by food, drink, or intimacy. It is the desire for more, for something beyond the world you know. I believe it is your desire for the divine. Your life's singular desire for milk will one day proliferate into a number of different desires: physical, social, sexual, religious. But now they are one desire angled in my milky direction. And why wouldn't your proto-religious desire be directed toward me if I am like a god to you? I am the only divinity you know. So I take your voracious appetite for milk, not as a sign of sinfulness, but as an image of potential love for the divine. I take you, in your moments of milk-drunk bliss, white dribbles rolling down cheeks and chin, catching in the folds of your neck, to be an image of beatific happiness.

I look at your small body with your large desires and wonder again what kind of baby God was. Did God also babble and kick with excitement? Did God reach out with chubby arms toward mother Mary? Did God smile while sleeping? What was God's first word? And what, I wonder again, about God sharing Mary's milk? Was God loathe to share mother's milk in the same way all other babies and toddlers are?

The infant's reluctance to share the nursing mother heralds the toddler's protest of her mother holding other babies. As both baby and toddler, you have yet to learn hospitality. Your desire for milk and mother has been laced with anxiety. You act as if other babies are threats, a habit that for many people persists well beyond infancy. I take your aggravation about sharing to speak both to an anxiety about scarcity in the material world and also to the inadequacy of that world to meet the intensity of your desire. You are drawn by material stimuli but not fully satisfied by those stimuli. Once your world opens more fully to the divine, you will find objects worthy of your strong desire. And learning to share—to choose friendship over immediate gratification— will be important to entering into that larger world where your desires can be met. So I want for you to learn to live into the generosity of your body, the very one that gave me fetal cells to tend my injured sites. I want you to learn to give and receive the love of others beyond your mother-god, to open the gates of your small kingdom to welcome those who seem strange competitors for the earthly goods around you.

For a few months, everything goes well. I provide the milk you take; you take the milk you need, just as Augustine described it. I am an image of divine bounty to you, and my body signifies the unending gifts of God. It is good. Then one day, as I feel myself overwhelmed by the stress of academic work and child-raising and household management, my body stops making enough. The babysitter brings you to me hungry, and after a minute of suck-ling, you begin to suckle desperately, then cry in frustration. I try different postures and techniques for generating more milk for you. Eventually you become quiet, if not content. I give you back to the babysitter. An hour later, you are hungry again, back at my breast, and we repeat the same discomfiting ritual. When I take you to the doctor two days later, she tells me your weight has dropped. We develop a plan to increase my milk supply, and she gives the plan a 50 percent chance of success. Formula is our plan for failure. I hear the word formula as if she has recommended poison. Anxiety fills me.

I become feverish in my attempts to revive my milk supply. For seven days I nurse and then pump every hour, waking up twice more at night to do the same, while still trying to keep up at work. I eat oatmeal and lactation cookies and give up exercise. I spin myself into worry and exhaustion, and everyone around me— your father, my students, our friends—feels it. The day I give you formula, I cry. You take the formula happily. I remain unconsoled.

Eventually, the milk supply builds back up. It is never as plen-tiful as before, but it is enough as you begin to eat solid foods. We continue nursing, though it's not easy, and I often feel guilty and annoyed. Why do I not release myself from my nursing anxiety to love you by other means? I have become confused about my significance—as if my milk were love itself, the abundant life you drink down in liquid form.

How many days did I deny you satiation out of my desire to reclaim my role as the abundant milk-giver? What kind of love was this that kept you hungry? I am disturbed by the violence of my love. The slip from loving to harming is easier and subtler that I had imagined.

Sara Ruddick tells a story about a mother who loves her baby who will not sleep. The mother is left largely on her own with her baby, who cries through long days and short nights, until the mother is nearly crazed with sleep deprivation. One night as she wakes, stupefied, to more screams and tears from her infant, she stumbles into the child's room and tries to comfort her baby. Holding the baby in her arms, she imagines herself throwing it through the window, the glass shattering around her. The vision is so real she believes she has done it for a moment. Horrified, terrified, she takes the baby out and rides public transportation all night, keeping herself and her baby in view of others. As the guilt-ridden mother recounts this story to a group of mothers, one of them says to her that she did all she could to keep her baby safe and that what she did was enough. She and the baby survived the night.

I try to practice this same compassionate response to my own story. I tell myself that I did what was needed. I took you to the doctor; I did not leave your nutrition up to my own judgments; I did give you formula when you needed it. I kept you safe. Even so, today I long to feed that hungry, crying infant. Of course, I can't reach into the past and undo my frantic decisions. I am not God who holds all of time in my being. Now I can only pray that the Creator of time and babies and milk will be present to that suffering babe that you once were—and to her suffering mother, too.

I pray that the mother that I once was will know that however much my milk-giving expresses life and love, life and love are still distinct from my milk. It is not my milk that holds you in being, gives you life, or saves you. I have confused the image with imaged—milk with love, myself with life-giver.

It can be a fine line, to love the image as a way of loving the imaged, and to love the image instead of the imaged. It is easy to peel the two apart, separating image from imaged, creation from Creator, and so to seek in the first what can only be satisfied in the second. Confusing the two, I plunged us both into misery. For you are not my creation but God's gift to me, and as a gift, you are a source of sweet delight. May I know you as a gift of the Creator, as a sign of divine love, an image of grace. Your father and I have spoken, and it is time for you to have another mother—Mother Church—and through her, to draw nearer to Mother God. We call our family and church to set a date for your baptism.

CHAPTER 2

Imitation

*You gathered me together from the state of disintegration
in which I had been fruitlessly divided. I turned from
unity in you to be lost in multiplicity.*

In their perverted way, all humanity imitates you.

It is your baptism day, and you are asleep in my arms. As Mass
ends, not even the joyful strains of the closing hymn wake you.
In the back of the church is the font where you will be baptized
in a smaller service. I walk slowly toward it, thinking about a bib-
lical story I will one day tell you: the story of two sisters, Mary
and Martha, as they host Jesus at their home in Bethany—one
of Scripture's better-known episodes.

When Jesus visits the women, Martha bustles about, cooking
and tidying and carrying out the traditional duties of hospitality.
It is hard work, made more onerous as the heat from the oven
and the energy of preparation condense into a cloud of swelter-
ing effort. Martha wipes some sweat off her forehead and pauses
to look at her sister, sitting raptly at Jesus's feet, drinking in his

words as if they are life itself. Isn't this how it has always been? She, shouldering their heaviest responsibilities, as Mary moves lightly through life? She, grinding, kneading, washing, sweeping, scurrying, fussing—as Mary loses herself in prayer? Martha has put up with Mary's selfishness—or obliviousness, whatever it is—her whole life, but not today, not during this visit of their dear friend and rabbi.

Irritation mounting, Martha itches to expose her sister's sin, even to humiliate her in front of their guest. She blurts out her complaint: "Jesus, don't you see Mary is doing nothing? Tell her to help me!" Exposed, her rage melts into embarrassment. What did she expect Jesus to do? Lecture Mary like a child? His rebuke is gentle. "Martha, Martha, you are worried and distracted by many things; there is need of only one thing."

It is a hard story for many of us, this tale of two sisters, but I have learned that monks, by and large, love it. They read it as an allegory of the active life and the contemplative life. Mary is a figure of contemplation, concerning herself with the one needful thing: prayer. Her stillness is the way of true knowledge and perfect holiness. Martha is the active life, busy with many things. Telling the tale to a novice, an old monk whips a well of water into a frenzied whirlpool and calls the novice to see his reflection in it. "I cannot," the novice replies. "That is right; now wait," the old monk responds. As the pool settles and becomes placid, the old monk calls the novice to look into it again. Now the novice can see his reflection staring back at him. "And so it is with your soul," the old monk says. "To see in your spirit a reflection of God, the waters of your soul must be still." Where Mary is clear, gathered, singular, Martha is befogged, spilt, and scattered. Mary is the calm, reflective pool; Martha, the unquiet water.

I think of this story, and the monk's interpretation of it, as I stare at the pool of water now in front of me, your baptismal font.

Dissipation and multiplicity are common metaphors for how sin wrecks a person, how it fractures a person's identity and keeps her from wholeness, health, and integrity. They are certainly two of Augustine's primary images. What mother wants that for her child? I pray your spirit will be like Mary's, stilled by attention to the one thing that is needful. I pray your self will be calm as the water before me, reflecting your divine image. I pray God will save you from dissipation.

You nestle in my arms, dressed in white, encircled by family, friends, and godparents all in their Sunday best. What will you make of this event when you see photos someday? What does God make of it? This morning's sacramental rite seems so unlike the baptism of Jesus. We wait in an ornamented church, not out in the wilderness; before a high and shallow font, not by a storied river. You are still a babe in arms, not an adult preparing for his life's ministry. Even so, this ceremony is one of the forms in which baptism has come to us across the centuries. This is how the church imitates the baptisms of Scripture. It is intriguing how imitation upon imitation has, over the years, led to such transformation. Imitation is a queer and ambivalent act.

There is a way of thinking of both Martha's work and Mary's rest as different ways of imitating the God who never stops working good things and who is at the same time rest itself. But one merits rebuke, while the other models the perfect life for centuries of monks. What is the difference?

I wonder if Martha's imitation of divine hospitality is perverse because it leaves no room for God's actual presence. Her activity, not Christ's presence, becomes the center around which the visit turns for her, as her preparations take up all the space and air, banishing any whiff of worship. Her feverish attempts to imitate God have blinded her to God's presence in her home. It seems clear in the monastic retelling the stakes of the difference between false and true imitation of God: perverse imitation leads to a disintegrated self, lost in multiplicity; good imitation gathers the self into a unified desire.

The circle gathered around the font radiates excitement, and you awake. You are delighted by the font of water, which is still as glass. Breaking its surface, I wet my hand to cross myself. Before I can bless you, you have dipped your own hand in the water and smacked it to your head. I smile at you. You grin back with a happy exhale that is almost a laugh. Then you wiggle down and try to stand like me and all the other adults around you. I give you a few moments to crawl around as my mind drifts away from the font to the brunch plans afterwards. Your father will pick up the food; I will go home with your godparents and grandparents. Have I given him the order number? Do we have enough cups and plates at home? I *think* I remembered to take the cake out of the refrigerator. You are clamoring for more holy water now, and so, my Martha-like planning interrupted, I pick you up and bless you. The baptism is about to begin.

Watching you copy the gestures of the adults gathered, my mind rings with words I read recently. "Right from the first days of life, every healthy human being is avidly monitoring those nearby, learning to recognize, interpret, and even imitate their expressions. An innate capacity for empathizing with others becomes apparent within the first six months." Soon it will be the words of Scripture and prayer that fill our room, but in these quiet moments, I think of this observation from Sarah Hrdy. What are you doing when you imitate me crossing myself? What is it you see as you recognize, interpret, and copy? What do you learn as you attempt to empathize with me?

Hrdy writes of an experiment in the 1970s in which a developmental psychologist made a series of silly faces in front of newborns, some as young as twelve hours old, one as young as forty-two minutes. When alert and attentive, the newborns imitated the psychologist as he made faces at them. He stuck out his tongue, and the infants did, too. He opened his mouth wide; the babies did the same. He pursed his lips as if kissing the air, and the infants made the same air-kissing expression back at him. The psychologist's findings astonished Hrdy and most of the scientific community. How could one so young know how to imitate facial expressions? How could an hours-old infant already be moving toward a capacity to empathize?

All the more surprising was an experiment undertaken a couple of decades later. In this second experiment, a different psychologist made faces at a chimp rather than a human infant. Abandoned by his mother, this chimp was human-raised. At five weeks, the chimp, like the newborn human, imitated her psychologist, sticking out her tongue, opening her mouth wide, and protruding her lips. The chimp baby continued imitating the human until she was twelve weeks, at which point she seemed to lose all interest in imitation. She stopped responding to the silly faces. A rhesus monkey followed a similar arc, at first imitating like the human newborns did but growing weary of the game by day seven. But humans tread a different course. We become more interested in imitating after twelve months and much better at imitating around twenty-four months. Though imitation seems instinctive to many apes, human imitation differs in that it grows in toddlerhood. What could account for this divergence? Hrdy's explanation is fascinating. The maturing of the imitation impulse in humans is funded, she argues, by empathy. Toddler humans imitate because they desire to know one another, because, as Hrdy writes, "A human child is born eager to connect with others." While apes remain profoundly self-centered, humans develop what Hrdy calls "other-regarding tendencies."

So the story about imitation is this: like all primates, human babies imitate; unlike them, their imitation is deepened and extended by their desire to connect with others. And so, by imitation, we learn to be human. We pass on our knowledge, our social behaviors, and our sinfulness. We pass on our hopes and efforts for redemption. We become human through attempting to become like our mothers.

But it is not just our mothers we imitate, nor only mothers who raise children. Throughout evolutionary history, the human mother is supported by a wider circle of caregivers. The small tribe gathered around your baptismal font suggests the type of parenting employed by humans and their hominin ancestors. They are your alloparents, and their role is to help rear the babe—you in this case—to maturity, a process called cooperative breeding. About two million years ago, it became necessary for hunter-gatherer mothers to enlist help provisioning their children, a tendency only made more urgent as human babies acquired larger brains and bigger heads, intensifying the need for more postpartum maternal help. Alloparents helped fill that gap.

Many, though not all, of your alloparents are standing around the baptismal font. Those gathered are close family members and friends who have already helped care for you, and who will care for you in the future. We are still in some ways our hominin ancestors, kin to our primate family. But how could we be identical with them? We live in a world that puts new pressures on the relations between parents and alloparents. You were born into a world inundated by books, studies, articles, and seminars about parenting. We learn from experts the myriad ways that alloparents may endanger you—by putting you to sleep on your stomach, by laying you on a soft mattress, by provisioning you in a manner considered wise and normal when your grandparents were having babies but no longer so today. Unlike my ancestors, I cannot receive the wisdom of experienced parents without first inspecting it, holding it up to the light of the experts of today for appraisal and judgment.

We have gained much through scientific advances—the rate of infants suddenly and mysteriously dying is less than a third what it was in 1990—but it has also disrupted our dependence on family and friends, especially those from older generations. The culture of experts has intervened in our former alloparenting rituals, lacing our gratitude to them with suspicion. Will you hold me in suspicion someday? Will you look at me as one committed to old-fashioned ideas, one who helped you pass the treacheries of infancy and childhood largely out of sheer, inexplicable luck?

There are other ways our alloparenting practices have changed over time. Baptism, as the church's ritualized form of alloparenting, names a relatively recent addition to human alloparenting practices. In baptism, we choose alloparents to provision not your body, but your spirit. The people who are becoming your godparents today are charged with a special investment in you. We want godparents who will pray for you, care for your soul, nurture you in your life with God. We want their faith to stand in for yours and assist your own faith in coming to maturity. They are your soul-mother and soul-father. They are exemplars for you to imitate.

So much we aspired to, anyway. How often does anyone choose godparents with pure regard for the child's soul? The practice of naming godparents inevitably becomes alloyed with more practical considerations. Surely no one, for example, chose Vito or Michael Corleone as his child's godfather because his faith in the God of Love was particularly inspiring. They were chosen because they could position their godchildren well in the world.

In a different story—one you will no doubt learn well before you know *The Godfather*—Cinderella's godmother comes as a fairy who transforms the material conditions of Cinderella's life, securing a gorgeous dress, romantic opportunity, and a shot at serious social mobility. It is a vision of godparenting where the godparent is an important source of provision, but in a way different from soul-parents. Godparents chosen for such provisioning, to advance a child's status in the world and help ensure her material success, serve less like shepherds of the child's soul and more like potential on-ramps to a better life. They become instruments for augmenting the child's—and perhaps even the parents'—power and influence in the world. At least that temptation cannot be far away when pragmatic concerns govern the practice of choosing godparents. But to choose godparents as soul-parents requires surrendering a certain fantasy of control over one's child. In choosing people to parent your soul, I dispel the illusion (however imperfectly, or temporarily) that you belong wholly to me. In baptism, I publicly declare that you have another family now.

This other family is a sign of your deepest, truest parentage. You are a child of God. Your godparents are a sign of the God who is your Mother and your Father. I am not the sole source of your life. My milk foreshadowed the soul-marking liquid in the font before us now. Through my milk, you received life. Through this water, you receive life abundant. I pray as you are baptized that your capacity to desire begin to grow in scope and complexity, that you will learn to pursue goods more remote, less immediately gratifying, and yet more fulfilling.

The moment of your baptism has come. I pass you to your godmother, and you, bewildered but enchanted by the candles, acquiesce to the ritual. The priest prays for you, invoking saints connected to your name, your family, and your godparents. With these saints, he enlarges your circle of alloparents still further. Your godmother tilts you back toward the font, as the priest scoops some water for the first of three dousings. The waters of baptism pour over your tender scalp once, twice, three times, as the Spirit clothes you in Christ, who gives you new kinship to Christ's Father—invoking the Triune God who is your divine Mother.

What does baptism mean for my relationship to you? I am, in a way, displaced. No longer am I your sole mother—if I ever was. You have a godmother and a Mother Church, and so my claim on you is mitigated by these claims I have invited others to make on you. The ritual of baptism underscores your strangeness to me, the way you are not mine. You have your own soul, separate from mine, growing and changing on a pilgrimage that is your own. But if there is a new strangeness between us, there is also a new kinship: we are sisters now, sisters with a common parent.

I think of your special saint, the one we especially ask to pray for you, Macrina—and her mother, Emmelia, too. Someday, after I tell you about Mary and Martha, I will tell you about them, too. I will tell you about how Macrina was so close to her mother that Emmelia joked that while she bore all her other children for the usual nine months, Macrina she carried about with her always and everywhere. I will tell you about how when Macrina's father died, she convinced Emmelia to turn their home into a monastery. They freed their servants to live in equality with them and invited other women to join them, too. Macrina became, in a way, her mother's spiritual mother. This was a transformation Emmelia herself encouraged by agreeing to take direction from her daughter and so become her daughter's spiritual daughter. What a strange passage that must have been for Emmelia! Or maybe it did not seem strange to her at all. Perhaps it was simply the culmination of a transformation that had been going on for years, as Macrina was coming into her own forceful presence as an adult. After all, it was not as if in the process of assuming their new roles, the two women left behind their biological ties. How could they?

One of the stories about them highlights their new relationship, in both its spiritual and biological dimensions. Macrina had a small tumor in her breast but refused, out of modesty, to see a doctor. To modern sensibilities, it sounds backwards and prudish, one more apparent battle between religion and science. To my motherly sensibilities, it sounds horrifying—as it did to Emmelia's. I cannot imagine watching you refuse treatment for what would almost certainly have been a life-ending affliction, nor could Emmelia imagine that for her daughter. Macrina, however, had reasons for her decision. She lived in a world where women's lives were shaped by the fear of assaults and forced marriages. Emmelia was herself thwarted in her hope of holy virginity because her father determined that her beauty made her vulnerable to precisely such dangers. Marriage to a good man gave Emmelia a measure of safety. Macrina's life nearly repeated her mother's, except that when her fiancé died, she was able to convince her parents not to betroth her again. Who can blame her, then, after living under the specter of violent male lust, for resisting her mother's entreaties to bare her breast to a strange man?

Devoted as Macrina was to her mother, she could not ignore Emmelia's pleas. Weeping, she went to pray. She rose from prayer with mud in her hands, made from mingling the earth on which she prostrated herself with the tears she shed. She went to Emmelia with the salve and asked her to cover the tumor with it and sign the cross over it. Emmelia did, and Macrina's breast was healed, a tiny scar marking the site of the miracle even after her death.

This is, I think, a beautiful example of a biological relationship transformed by the spiritual. Macrina revered her mother even as she found her conscience would not yield to her mother's appeals. She practiced a devoted disobedience. I pray that like Emmelia, I will be gracious enough to receive your own sisterly wisdom, and that like Macrina, you will be courageous enough to share it with me. I pray that I will be willing to become your daughter and you my mother. I hope, when the time comes, that I will be willing to imitate you as you are so willing now to imitate me.

But what if you make decisions that are not wise? What did Monica suffer, watching Augustine throw himself into a life that he describes as dissipated in pleasure? Writing from the perspective of older age, Augustine claims that God was speaking to him through his mother's warnings about adultery, but at the time, her advice seemed to him "womanish." For years, she prayed and waited for Augustine to come to the God she loved. At the same time, Monica, like so many parents, tailored her advice to the needs of her son's career. She did not immediately press marriage because she did not want to hold him back from assuming the social status she believed he might one day achieve. Monica tolerated his less than chaste behavior, his dubious friendships, his wanderings through another religion. She had a theological escape hatch for him, after all: baptism, which was delayed so that it might wash away the youthful sins she prayed would pass.

So Monica prayed and waited. How many mothers wait in hope that their children will come around to a better way, a higher virtue, a richer life? And how many are disappointed? Monica's patience was rewarded as Augustine matured and submitted to baptism and holy orders. She became his sister in the faith, as Emmelia did with Macrina, and they share together a spiritual vision in Ostia. She dies before seeing her son become a priest and bishop, but she must have seen that he was on that path. In the end, things worked out well for Monica, at least in terms of her hopes for her son. Still, for a time, their life together lingers in their difference, in an estrangement of vision. The threat of perpetual separateness without spiritual kinship hovers over his adolescence and young adulthood.

I feel the threat of our own perpetual separateness, even on the day of your baptism. Although I was baptized, it was not into your church. I was baptized in a Protestant church. I still am Protestant. Our churches recognize each other's baptisms. We were both baptized into the Trinity, and in that way, our baptisms are a sign of our unity despite their location in different churches. We try, as a family, to create some kind of unity of church life, attending two different services each week, Mass on Saturday evening, service on Sunday morning. But a child has to be baptized into a particular church, and we have baptized you into the Roman Catholic Church. You are now a part of this Church in a way that I am not, a division I reflect on and re-enact each Mass as I remain seated during the Eucharist. And the Catholic Church will now be your mother.

I have given you to this mother willingly, gladly, but my relationship with your Mother Church is complicated. The Catholic Church is not my mother. So I have given you, my beloved, over to a different family. What will happen as you grow? Will you one day take the Eucharist, leaving me seated alone each Mass? Will we become spiritually alien as we also become spiritually kin? How did your baptism become a sign of our disunity as well as our unity?

After your baptism, after you emerge from the waters of chaos to eat strawberries and lemon cake, after all the godparents, grandparents, and friends have gone their separate ways, I am left wondering about baptism, especially about Jesus's baptism. It was John, of course, who baptized Jesus and inaugurated his ministry. Because of this, he is the forerunner of Christ, the one who says to the son of his mother's kinswoman, *I must decrease so thou might increase.*

John's declaration resonates with me. In some ways, I see myself as your forerunner, the one pointing to you and saying that I must decrease that you might increase. That is what parenthood is, a series of diminishments so that you may come into your own as a separate person. There is the literal diminishment of a body growing smaller after pregnancy. And there is the more difficult diminishment, in which I learn when and how to pull back my own will so that yours can come into its own. When you were in my womb, my will substituted for yours; you were nourished when I was nourished. I determined where your body was at all times by determining where my own body was. Once you were born, I learned to read your cues for hunger and thirst, to read these stirrings of a growing will, but I still decided where to put you, when to change you, how long to feed you. As you get older, you become independent of my body for nourishment, and I learn to give you choices, early exercises that let you practice what it might be like to will the good. Eventually you will not need me at all.

John and Mary: the forerunner who points to Jesus and the God-bearer who gives birth to him. Both point to Jesus, and Jesus learns from both of them. Like John, Jesus baptizes and speaks of God's kingdom. Yet he also goes beyond John. He inaugurates a baptism into his own life, death, and resurrection, and he is the kingdom he proclaims. Similarly, Jesus imitates Mary. In Gethsemane, he says yes to the Father; on Golgotha, he gives birth to new life. The yes and birth-giving of Jesus is realized on the cross, where he bears all of us to new life in God. These are transformed imitations that show new depths of the imitated act, and they issue from the love of both the imitated one and the imitated act. By these imitations, Jesus comes to take his place in the world. Through them, he comes to his saving work for the world.

You, too, imitate your forerunners—constantly, insistently. As I write, you come up to me, thirsty. I pour you some water and get myself a can of sparkling water. I sit down beside you to drink and work. You begin to gulp greedily, but observing me, you grow dissatisfied with your cup. You want my can. My attempts to persuade you otherwise lead to angry protests. You want to do as I do, drink water as I drink water, be human as I am human. You throw down your sippy cup with all the mightiness of a toddler's anger. It leaks water onto the kitchen floor, making a small puddle by the table as I sit amazed at this display of frustration. You snatch at my can, crumpling its side as you do. I put my can away and you burst into uncontainable sobs. You, my recently baptized baby, are now making a fuss over a different kind of water. You want the water of human life, the water you see at the lips of your beloved. Comforting you with kisses, I take out a cup of water like yours and sit at your small table to drink it with you. We are the same; I do as you do. You are momentarily appeased.

You pursue your humanity so passionately. Your desire to join us creatures who care for you, to become like us, is a force, like gravity or magnetism or electricity. I watch as your desire to be human makes you human. Your humanity is born from your love of humans.

But how do I teach you what to emulate and what not to, what is right for your age and what is right only for me as an adult? You are indiscriminate in your imitation. Sometimes that leads you into humor (your favorite joke of putting on my shoes). Other times imitation leads you into danger (your recent attempt to wield my kitchen knife).

What are you imitating when you imitate me? Are you imitating me as your caretaker and one of your species? As the one who images God to you? Or both? If you are imitating me as your proxy for the divine, then when is that problematic and when laudatory?

Augustine is convinced that all sin can be described as a false imitation of God. When he stole the pears as a boy, as he later writes, he attempted to show himself above any law, and so imitate the God who is subject to no one. In this way, the pear theft is paradigmatic of all sin. Augustine runs through a litany of sins, describing the perfections of God they perversely imitate. In our perversity, Augustine writes, all humanity imitates God. But of course we imitate in our perversity. Where else could we be? We are steeped in the perversities of shallow love. But that cannot mean all imitation is perverse. Martha's soul-scattering imitation of God's work is not the same as Mary's soul-gathering imitation of God's rest. Augustine's imitation of God in his pear theft is not the saint's imitation of God's love.

We are called to be like God in so many ways—generosity, humility, patience, goodness. But then there are other ways we clearly ought not attempt to be like God, ways that lead finite creatures to narcissism or isolation or dissipation. We cannot, for example, sustain the universe, however busy we make ourselves, and we will likely do great damage to ourselves and others in the attempt. So how is the desire to be like God rightly pruned, corrected, redirected? It can so easily turn from a desire to be united with God to a desire to displace God—from a desire to be near God to a desire to be far from God. How can I help you learn to imitate well? How can I learn myself how to imitate well?

When I hold you, I often feel your barely coordinated fingers stroking my arm, as you have felt me do to you for months now. You are learning my way of love. I hope you will improve upon it, that you will make it deeper, truer, richer. But my lack of love becomes your own, too. You are learning about possessiveness from me. I tried to teach you about the commonness of God's gifts when I offered you for baptism, but now you are learning not all water is as shared as the pool in that font. When I take my can from your grasp, I say, "That is Mommy's water. Your water is right here." You have learned from me to claim things. "My's, my's!" has become a familiar cry of yours that makes me both smile and resolve to teach you about sharing. In teaching you to share, I must become my own pupil.

And then there are ways that I pass on my pathologies and those of our age because I cannot find another way to live. "Hurry,

hurry! Where are your shoes? It's time to go, go, go! We're going to miss the beginning!" What unsettles me about these moments is that I am actively imparting anxiety to you, instilling in you some inner tic that makes you obey clocks and commands as readily as I do, as most adults do. I know some day these sins will revisit me. One future day of reckoning, you will be older, and you will look at me (resentful? wounded? matter-of-fact?) and explain how successful I was in teaching you anxiety.

This world, it sometimes seems, is not made for children. Maria Montessori says that there are two poles of humanity, the child and the adult. The child is ordered toward internal ends, clustered around building the adult she will become. The adult, meanwhile, lives in the world of external ends, building things outside her own person. An adult walks up the stairs because she needs to get something on the second floor; a child walks up the stairs for the joy in the effort in doing so. Montessori cautions that these two poles of humanity must be kept in check, neither dominating nor suppressing the other. As I hurry you about and teach you to live by clocks and technologies, I realize that I am forcing you to live by adult codes. Even when I agree with your rebellion against the codes, I enforce them.

We have finished our water now, and I have turned back to work. I know that you want my attention, but like many mothers, I am doing many things. I am collecting dishes into our sink. I am chopping pears for your lunch tomorrow. I am listening for the laundry to finish. I am scribbling notes for my seminar the next day. You begin to fuss, and I accelerate my pace. You want to be held and kissed and stroked, but I am committed to my tasks. You will be there when I finish, I tell myself. I cannot bring myself to break away.

We are playing a game of Mary and Martha: I, the adult, ordered to goals, functions, and purpose; you, the child, ordered to attachment, pleasure, and intimacy. We are Montessori's two poles of humanity, our differences pulling us in separate directions. I have closed my eyes and ears to your desires, enclosing myself in my adulthood and so, at the same time, scattering my soul. Even as I attempt to distract you with bits of food or toys or song, you keep calling to me. You will not be diverted from your desire. You are standing on your tiptoes now, arms outstretched, repeating "mama" with undiminished longing. My pace accelerates still faster. Just a bit more time, I tell myself. I fumble in my haste, cracking a dish, spoiling my notes, slicing my finger. Blood stains the fruit. Your cries finally pierce my willed deafness. I am doing many things, but there is only one thing you want. I stop. I take you in my arms. I kiss your teary cheeks. As I sway and shush and soothe us both, your small body warms my chest. I close my eyes and, for the next few moments, imitate your singleness of desire.

CHAPTER 3

Mercy

Why is it that a person should wish to experience suffering
by watching grievous and tragic events which he himself
would not wish to endure? Nevertheless he wants to suffer
the pain given by being a spectator of these sufferings,
and the pain itself is his pleasure.... But what quality of
mercy is it in fictitious and theatrical inventions?

I am listening to the radio and driving to work when the morn-ing news program pivots to another story of a suffering child. As the report turns grim, I breathe deeply, blink hard, and stab the power switch. I pass the rest of the commute in silence, exor-cising mental images and tidying mascara smudges.

It has become a familiar ritual since you were born—since before you were born, really. When I was pregnant, I blamed my weepiness on hormones, as if that somehow distanced me from my sadness. But long after your birth, my tears are eas-ily provoked. When I am alone at home, I sometimes give in to them, blubbering at terrible stories of children neglected, abused, war-ravaged, or rejected, while I fry eggs or unload the dishwasher.

What is it that makes me cry when I hear such stories? They are horrible stories, but there were horrible stories before you existed, and I rarely cried then. Do I now imagine you in the situations of these children? Am I responding to the possibility that terrible things *could* happen you? Or have I, through you, learned to love other children more?

I don't know how to explain my increased sensitivity to suffering children, but I know I am not unique in it. It is a dark mystery of motherhood, the difficulty of listening, dry-eyed, to stories of children in peril. I know one mother who gave away all her books in a once-beloved series because they included stories of ill-treated children. Another confessed she rarely listens to the news anymore. But I listen, sometimes turning away from particularly painful stories, or stories that might make me puffy-eyed and blotchy at work. In the meantime, you grow and grow. You are a small child now, and still I remain easily moved. I seem permanently altered in this regard. Because of you, the suffering of the world has become vivid to me.

Your existence has invited me deeper into the life of mercy. Before you were born, I thought I might love you as an extension of myself, or as I have loved other small children with whom I have joked and played. But sometime during my pregnancy, when I began to love you, I sensed this love was different, and the nature of my love clarified the moment your father placed you in my arms. My love for you, I knew then, was not only—not even principally—directed at your delightfulness, but at your vulnerability. I loved you because you were given me to love, because you depended on me for life. It is probably unwise, or nonsensical, to attempt to explain my love for you, as if it could be analyzed in causes and kinds, but inasmuch as "because" ever makes sense following a declaration of love, I can say that I loved you because without my love, you would die.

The moment of receiving a child who elicits mercy and converts the caregiver to a new life is narrated in some of my favorite stories. George Eliot explores one such conversion in *Silas Marner*, as the miserable miser Silas is robbed of the gold that is his sole source of pleasure, only to meet a golden-haired toddler in need of a parent. As he opens his life and possessions to her, he finds a path to repaired trust and renewed community. Eliot puts it with pleasing conciseness, "There was love between him and the child that blent them into one, and there was love between the child and the world." When Silas responds to the child in mercy, she in her love opens the world to him.

A bleaker version of this tale is told by the South African film (also a novel) *Tsotsi*. The titular hero begins life as a street child and becomes a gang leader. Tsotsi is also a thief and murderer who kills without thought and seemingly without feeling. His eyes are cold and hard. After a car robbery, he discovers he has kidnapped a baby who had been in the backseat. The baby is helpless; he can only cry and trust his needs will be fulfilled. Encountering this child—meeting, in the words of Roger Ebert, "eyes more demanding than his own"—Tsotsi is transformed. Only a flicker of mercy remains in him when he discovers the babe, but the helplessness of that creature fans the flame of that love, which illumines his life in a hopefulness that upends and transforms his criminal existence. By gunpoint, he enlists the help of a nursing woman named Miriam (I think of Moses). In his encounter with the child, Tsotsi's world does not get set right, nor does he become perfectly virtuous. The hope of his story is very near despair; it ends with a police officer pointing a gun at Tsotsi as he tries to return the baby to its parents, his hands up. In a world more alert to images of unarmed black men and boys, hands up, facing officers with guns, the ending is even more despairing now than when the movie was first released over a decade ago. But the hope is still there. The audience does not know how Tsotsi's encounter with the police ends, but they do see Tsotsi learn to love and suffer for that love. Less determined by the violence surrounding him, Tsotsi has become freer, more human.

Like those of Silas Marner and Tsotsi, my own initial experience of merciful love for a baby, for you, was powerful. That first moment I held you was like a miracle. It was a conversion. But there is potential danger to such merciful love, as I experienced it. If it fails to open up to other types of love, it becomes oppressive, pathological, even death-dealing. Here is one way: in loving mercifully, a person can become attached to an experience of herself as merciful. She can take pleasure in her own mercifulness and wrongly perpetuate the neediness that calls forth her mercy—which then becomes false.

I've heard a story about a particularly perverse case like this. A mother cared for her sick child for years, sacrificing socially and financially to care for her wheelchair-bound daughter, who was afflicted with multiple mysterious conditions. And then one day, after the child had become a young adult, she partnered with a young man and killed her mother. She declared she was not sick, not wheelchair-bound, in need of no special treatment, and never had been. The mother had made her complicit in a charade—had even deceived the daughter about her own health—since the child was an infant. The young man was her secret boyfriend she had met through a concealed social media account. From prison, the daughter said of her mother, "She would have been the perfect mom for someone that was actually sick. But I'm not sick. There's that big, big difference."

It's an awful, twisted story. Who identifies with the mother? Who would want to? But as repulsive as that mother seems to me, I see something familiar in her. I recognize a faint similarity between the pleasure I take in your need for me, and the pathological pleasure this mother took in her caregiving. Of course, the mother's mercy was neither healthy nor true. It had petrified. Her mercy referred to itself rather than her child who was its supposed object. So hollowed, her mercy became a form of hatred. But it began in and still bore some distorted resemblance to true mercy.

Can I purse my lips and shake my head in melancholy judgment, disavowing any affinity with this woman's temptation to find strange pleasure in mercy? You are getting so big now; you need me less and less. You like to tell me "nope" and run away when I ask you to come. You want to do everything by yourself. Constantly now you assert and perform your independence. But sometimes, you need me more than you want your independence. Something will scare you—thunder, a rowdy dog, an unknown person—and you run with trembling lip, calling out to me. Is it perverse that those moments are so sweet to me? I love to provide you refuge. You stretch out your arms saying "mama," and I wrap your growing body in a giant hug and feel your heartbeat begin to steady as my presence sets your world right again.

What kind of happiness is it that I experience in these moments? Am I enjoying the importance that your need gives me, subtly taking pleasure in your pain? Is this mercy malignant, kin to the mother's with the not-sick child? Or do I treasure these moments because their infrequency underscores that you are growing to need me less and less? Do I honestly want you to be your best and healthiest self? I hope so. I'm afraid my love runs in both directions, that I'm overly attached to being merciful to you, even as I long for your health and wholeness. I know, at least, that there is less difference between the toxic mother and me than I want to believe; I catch scents of noxious, untrue mercy in myself. One difficult feature of mercy is that when it is true, it wants to be unnecessary. True mercy wants to blossom into pure delight.

If one movement of mercy is in hoping for its own diminishment, another must be toward its own expansion. The way of
charity that the child calls us to—that you call me to—is a way
that constantly magnifies, not because your needs multiply but
because you call me to be open to the needs of others. I once
had a teacher who spoke of how beauty promotes *lateral regard*.
When one loves a beautiful, fragile vase, she explained, one treats
it with special care. And then one begins to give special regard to
other fragile vases like it, and from there, to vases less like it, and
perhaps, eventually to all vases. Regard moves outward, laterally,
from the one admired object to multiple to many.

This seems to me true not just of vases, but of children as well.
In learning to love you, I'm opened to the beauty and vulnerability
of all children in a new way. It is not that you become interchangeable with any other child—I remain especially attuned to you,
the child who has been given particularly to me to love, in a way
that is powerfully singular—but the potency of that love inspires
more love, for other creatures like you. Envisioning a renewed
heaven and earth, the prophet Isaiah says that a little child shall
lead us. That little child might be Jesus, and it might also be any
child given to an adult to love. Any adult can follow her love for
a child into the way of merciful love for all creatures. The love for
the child can blend into the love for the world. In learning mercy
for you, I can become merciful to all the miserable.

Still, has that ever happened to any mother—to any caregiver—except Mother Mary? If you are an image of the Messiah
to me, coming to inaugurate me into the way of love, I am as often
your traitor as your disciple. My love for you is spiked with violence—the violence of anger, of possessiveness, of defensiveness.
Sometimes you bear my violence; sometimes other children do.

Scripture speaks of the motherly betrayal of mercy more than
once. There is that terrible story of the two mothers fighting over a

child after one of them has smothered her own child in her sleep. They come before Solomon to settle the child's true parentage. The king commands the living child be divided in two with the sword. One woman cries out the child should be given to the other woman rather than killed. The second woman would rather the child be cut in two than given to her rival. Solomon judges the first woman to be the true mother.

The story does not hold up today. It seems to me no particularly impressive display of wisdom—not, at least, if one interprets it as a story about determining biological parentage. Can we imagine a mother so twisted by anger and hatred that she would kill her own son rather than let another women have him? Yes. I think those of us who live in an age fascinated with stories of sensationally bad mothers can imagine such horrific violence. And can we imagine a woman who chooses the good of another woman's child, even at cost to herself? I hope we can imagine that scenario even more easily. So Solomon's test does not seem to me a fail-safe method for testing biological parentage. But if one takes it as a story about one's fitness to be a parent, it is more promising. Regardless of whether she gave birth to him, the woman who chooses the good of a child acts more like a mother to him. She follows the child into the way of mercy.

But the second mother, the untrue mother, testifies to how love for a child can be corrupted. The untrue mother is willing to let the child die if she cannot possess him. What is it about human life that our love can come so very near hate? I wonder if the intimacy of love and hate come from how love opens us to pain and suffering, and our attempts to foreclose this pain and suffering inevitably mutilate the love and wound the beloved. We can, like the untrue mother in the Solomon story, attempt to stifle our suffering by stamping out others' joy—or we can, like the mother of the child who was not truly ill, learn to take pleasure in our own relationship to another's suffering. Both are attempts to deny that love passes through suffering. Mercy, true mercy, is the name for that suffering—the suffering of sharing a loved one's suffering.

Often, you seem to press me toward greater mercy. I have been a vegetarian for some years now, which you began noticing when you were very young. When you asked why, I found it difficult to explain. I am not a purist about meat, but I try to avoid supporting systems I find deeply unjust. The meat industry, to my mind, is one such system. Abstract reasoning is difficult for a child, so again and again, we have this conversation, where you ask me why I do not eat meat and then cannot digest my answer. You are further mystified by the cases when I *do* eat meat—when served pasta Bolognese at a friend's table, for example, or in a recent bout of anemia. Occasionally, I also eat fish. All of this troubles you, for you have imitated me into vegetarianism while developing your own rationale: meat is animals that were alive once, and now they're dead.

Your father and I chuckle about this—the passion of your commitment and the starkness of its expression. But as you continue to repeat this reasoning and persist in questioning my exceptions to vegetarianism, a tremor of doubt quivers in the back of my consciousness. Meat *is* animals that were alive once, but now they're dead. I am not sure what to do with this recognition, but I cannot see meat or animals quite the same now. I do not make exceptions as easily as I used to. What is it you have taught me, or led me into?

I see an analogy in Augustine. Over the course of his life, Augustine's love of rhetoric was both a stumbling block to God and the desire that gave birth to love of God. In a similar way, my love for you can be something that closes in on itself, blocking me from other loves, or it can become my entrance into God's merciful heart. In the short term, reading Cicero's *Hortensius* turned Augustine off from Scripture, which seemed primitive by comparison. But there were deeper changes at work in him. As Augustine writes, "The book changed my feelings. It altered my prayers, Lord, to be towards you yourself. It gave me different values and priorities." It marked, in sum, a conversion, inflaming in Augustine a love for truth that he learned to be faithful to over the course of his life. I pray that you mark such a conversion in me, that I will learn to be faithful to the mercy you awaken in me.

Augustine is aware of the many ways mercy can become false. He writes of the false mercy he learned from the theater, where he goes to escape the sorry state of his soul. But he is baffled by his desire to escape suffering by watching people suffer in tragedies. Why desire to witness suffering he would never wish to undergo? When a person is a spectator of tragedy, Augustine writes, the character's pain can become a pleasure, captivating the theatergoer and holding her attention. What is this pleasure? It is the pleasure of being moved, of experiencing oneself as merciful without actually doing anything merciful. The mercy is hollowed out. It becomes theatrical.

This is not an intuitive critique of the arts today. Many have mounted defenses of literature and the arts by claiming they can help us inhabit another's point of view. The arts make us more empathetic, more broad-minded, more compassionate—so the defense runs. But if the proper response to the arts is to feel, discuss, and evaluate, then what kind of compassion are we really learning? Are we reducing mercy to an emotion, a virtue of right feeling rather than right doing? Are we teaching ourselves that what it means to be good is to have the right opinions, the right affections, or the right taste?

I worry about this in part because I worry about what I am doing when I listen to the news. What am I doing when I take in these stories of suffering children, and weep, and go back to making dinner? Am I training myself in a false response to suffering? Into a theatrical version of mercy? But then—what am I doing when I turn the radio off?

I think of Jesus visiting Mary and Martha, a different, much more sorrowful visit than the one of busyness and rivalry. The sisters had sent notice to Jesus about the critical condition of their brother Lazarus, "Lord, he whom you love is ill." Urgent as the message was, though, Jesus does not immediately go to Bethany. (His disciples, it seems, do not want him to go at all. They fear he may be stoned there.) Jesus delays for two days, arriving after Lazarus has died. He knows Lazarus will be dead—he even tells his disciples he is glad, for the sake of their faith, that Lazarus died before they arrive. And still he seems, in different ways, moved by both Martha and Mary's reports of their brother's death.

When he nears Bethany, Martha hurries out to Jesus, reproaching him with her sadness and reaffirming her hope in him by saying, "[E]ven now I know that God will give you whatever you ask of him." Jesus responds to her with a striking revelation of who he is: the resurrection and the life. In the midst of what must have been great emotional turmoil, she offers a statement of faith in reply, affirming her trust in him as the Messiah. It is a powerful interaction, among the most compelling in the gospels. But it is Jesus's encounter with Mary that has been, for Christians across the centuries, especially poignant.

Where Martha's restless energy drives her out to Jesus, to engage him and restore her faith in him, Mary's sadness weighs on her, keeping her at home. She goes to Jesus only when Martha returns and tells her Jesus is asking after her. Finding him in the same spot her sister did, she opens with her sister's same reproach. "Lord, if you had been here, my brother would not have died." But she does not meet him like Martha, searching his eyes for answers, breathless from a brisk walk. Mary is bent down, kneeling before him as she weeps these words. Her friends with her also weep. Seeing them, Jesus "is greatly disturbed in spirit and deeply moved." He asks about the tomb, and Mary's entourage invites him to follow them. Then comes the shortest verse in Scripture: Jesus wept.

Later he will reach the tomb, pray, and raise Lazarus from the dead. Resurrection seemed to have been his plan all along, from the moment he heard Lazarus was sick. But first he weeps. Why not go directly to the raising? Why wait to encounter Martha and Mary before proceeding to the tomb? Why weep with Mary? And why did seeing Mary's weeping cause him to weep? I want to tell you this story someday, and you will ask me why Jesus wept. What will I tell you?

When a boat of refugees sank in the Mediterranean in an attempt to arrive in Lampedusa, Italy, dozens died. The story has become familiar, yet another typical immigration tragedy, but Pope Francis did not want it to become any less urgent. He asked, in a homily:

> Has any one of us wept because of this situation and others like it? Has any one of us grieved for the death of these brothers and sisters? Has any one of us wept for these persons who were on the boat? For the young mothers carrying their babies? For these men who were looking for a means of supporting their families? We are a society which has forgotten how to weep, how to experience compassion—"suffering with" others: the globalization of indifference has taken from us the ability to weep! . . . [L]et us ask the Lord for the grace to weep over our indifference, to weep over the cruelty of our world, of our own hearts, and of all those who in anonymity make social and economic decisions which open the door to tragic situations like this. "Has anyone wept?" Today has anyone wept in our world?

Since Pope Francis's address, thousands more immigrants have died. The passage to Lampedusa is now the most dangerous immigrant passage in the world. Do we weep each time a boat sinks en route to Lampedusa? Each time an immigrant dies or is assaulted on the way to the United States? For every child separated from parents at the U.S.-Mexico border? What good are these tears? How are they more than moments of self-indulgence? What makes them any more than an expression of theatrical mercy?

Augustine, for his part, has an at best ambivalent relationship to tears. He usually writes regretfully of his own tears—his infant sobs of greed and revenge, his tears at theatrical tragedies, his excessive grief at a friend's death. He even wonders if crying for an hour at his mother's death betrays Christian hope. But he often commends his mother's tears. Describing a time when he practiced a non-Christian religious faith, Augustine writes of his mother's distress. She wept for him as a mother weeps for a dead child. Augustine writes, addressing God, "You heard her and did not despise the tears which poured forth to wet the ground under her eyes in every place where she prayed. You heard her." Sobbing her story of a wayward son to a bishop, Monica begs him to refute her son's unchristian beliefs. The bishop responds, irritated at her refusal to back down from her request, "Go away from me: as you live, it cannot be that the son of these tears should perish." Ignoring the irritation, Monica receives the words "as if they had sounded from heaven."

What is it about these tears—Monica's, Pope Francis's, Jesus's— that makes them tears of true mercy rather than tears of theatricality or self-indulgence? Is it because they are offered up as prayers? Monica sobs in prayer, but Pope Francis says nothing of prayer in his homily. Why would he exhort the faithful to weep rather than asking them to pray? What good are tears without words of prayer? I'm not sure, but I wonder whether the tears

Pope Francis wants are like votive offerings, ablutions for the divine. Perhaps they are small sacrifices of our hearts that cleanse us and cry out to the divine. Wordless prayers.

There is an important way in which theater differs from reports of events in the world. Though we often receive news as theater, as stories from lands and people so distant they seem like fiction, they are not made-up stories. Through words or weeping, we can pray for the immigrants from Lampedusa. What would it mean to pray for Antigone or Cordelia Lear? You often want to pray for your beloved blanket "Blankie" these days. Part of you, though I don't think all of you, believes Blankie is alive because you love her so much. But I cannot believe the same of Antigone and Cordelia—or Tsotsi. I know they are fictions. Does watching them and weeping over them train me into a false mercy, where I take pleasure in my feeling of mercy but perform no merciful action? How can my tears be offered as a sacrifice when I have chosen to consume a tragic story for entertainment? I am haunted by Tsotsi, and I do not know what to do about it.

What can I do but pray? I pray that this haunting will constitute itself in the world as mercy. I pray that I will have eyes to see Tsotsi and Antigone and Cordelia in this world, that I will find their likenesses and show them lovingkindness. I pray that as you have opened me to the helplessness and vulnerability of children, so you will open me to other forms of suffering. I hope you will give me eyes to see the humanity of the suffering ones I might otherwise have glanced past. And I pray that I will be present to their suffering, suffering with them, and offering what sacrifices of mercy I can. This tenderhearted presence is the love your tender body calls me to. Your way of mercy, I see it now, is a love acquainted with grief.

CHAPTER 4

Suffering

What madness not to understand how to love a human
being with awareness of the human condition!

We arrive home, triumphant and heavy with ice cream after celebrating your first play. You are still flushed with excitement, chattering on about the performance as I send you to get ready for bed. Your father and I are so happy for you, so proud that you have stood on a stage in front of a full audience.

Minutes later, I come in to your room, only to find it empty. Where have you gone? I turn to leave the bedroom but am stopped short by a strange sound: muffled sobs coming from the closet. Opening the door, I find you curled in the corner, sobbing as if you had lost your best friend.

For the last five days, you have spoken to us only of the play. You eagerly anticipated every practice; you left each reluctantly. This all surprised your father and me because you are so shy. Speaking and social interactions come hard for you, but still you loved theater camp. It emboldened you even to whisper a line on stage. And now, suddenly, this wonderful little world you had found dissolved. I let you cry and try to comfort you with talk of other plays, but for you in this moment, there is only one play, only one perfect theater-community that made you feel better than any other community ever had. As you, in your anguish, put it, "There will never be this group of people together again, not this exact group."

A few days later, you ask whether you can be in other plays. It will be so sad when they end, you tell me, but you want to do one anyway. To you, they are worth the sadness. Already you realize that some joys cannot be prized apart from suffering. Who are you becoming? As an infant, you had that boundless, loosely formed desire for me and milk. Over time, your desire has gained depth, complexity, and shape. Now you desire a joy that knows pain.

I recognize, in this episode, a turning in our life together. Up to this point, my role as your mother has been to reduce your pain and impose myself between you and the world. I have absorbed life's trials to give you a safe and happy space to grow. You have been like your father's seedlings, under a grow-light indoors, protected from harsh winds, hard rains, and hungry snails. But now you are making your way into a less buffered world, finding more of the world's beauty and discovering the way joy comes alloyed with suffering. My job at this point is to trust that the suffering of the world will not extinguish your joy and to recede, just a little, so that you can enter more deeply into the world.

When, where, and how much to recede—these are the thorny questions confronting me now. What kind of suffering should I ask you to face? The question, I know, is charged with the privilege of one who can choose not to face the deep suffering of the world. The sadness of a summer camp ending is not the daily grind of poverty and racism. You are a middle-class white girl, and you do not face the dangers of a child like, for example, Tsotsi. And I am seeing Tsotsi everywhere these days, his hands up, his life poised between the threat of its ending and the possibility of its going on.

The director of the film *Tsotsi* recorded three different endings for the movie. In one, Tsotsi escapes into the darkness; in another, he's shot by a police officer when he reaches to give a bottle to the crying baby. The official ending, with Tsotsi raising his hands up in a suspended moment, underscores Tsotsi's vulnerability and the ambivalence of the encounter. Things could go in any direction. Now there is news story after story about just that image—an unarmed black boy, his hands up—ending in death.

The images in the news today are all the more gutting for how unlike Tsotsi the victims are. They are not inadvertent kidnappers overcoming a criminal past. If they were, the image would speak to the condition of a small subset of black lives. But the image speaks to a threat of death that hangs over all black men and boys in America today—and women and girls, too. When poet Claudia Rankine asks her friend what it is like to be the mother of a black son, she replies, "The condition of black life is one of mourning." Rankine's words remind me of an icon I have recently been contemplating, called *Our Lady Mother of Ferguson and All Those Killed by Gun Violence*. Styled after the icons in which Mother Mary prays with her palms up and the Christ-child revealed in her womb, *Our Lady Mother of Ferguson* presents Mary as a black mother. The child within her is a front-facing silhouette, his red heart circled with thorns and gold, his hands raised, and his body marked by a gun site. With this image, the iconographer inscribes the stories of all mourning black mothers into the story of Mary suffering violence against her own child. The stories are both particular and universal.

Violence against black bodies has a long history in our country, and my city of Waco is currently confronting a small piece of that history that took place on its own soil. One hundred years ago, a young black man named Jesse Washington was lynched in front of the courthouse downtown. The legacy of that event and the racist conditions that caused it have stayed with Waco over the decades, even as the memory of it has been preserved only in certain sectors of the city. Many in the black community remember it, and interpret the path of Waco's devastating 1953 tornado as following the same route as the lynching mob—God's providential judgment for the grievous sins of the city. But in many parts of Waco, the lynching has been forgotten. Together with some graduate students and other members of the community, I have been helping to plan a pilgrim march and service for the anniversary of the lynching. How, though, do I expose you to this story—which, in its rawest form, includes allegations of rape, a body burned and dragged through the city, and a crowd that celebrated by taking photographs of the mutilated corpse? How do I tell you the story in a way that is both faithful to the event and fitting for a child? Or, how do I tell you a story that is true but not soul-crushing?

Telling true stories is only part—perhaps the smaller part—of the problem of how you are to face suffering. My friend quoted James Baldwin to me the other day, "White children, in the main, and whether they are rich or poor, grow up with a grasp of reality so feeble that they can very accurately be described as deluded—about themselves and the world they live in." The delusion is generated not just by historiographic omissions and re-narrations. It is also made from the false worlds I make for you in order to protect you from suffering, from the ways I shore you up against need and ensconce you in a life of privilege. Instead of giving away money freely to those in need, I set aside more for you to have a quality education and comfortable life. Instead of sending you to failing public schools that largely serve children of color and poverty in our community, I send you to a stable, homogenous school. Am I teaching you to take refuge in your privilege? To minimize or deny your vulnerability, even at the expense of others?

These decisions about money and education are born of love, but they risk betraying the very mercy that funds them. For if my response to your vulnerability is to cut you off from the vulnerable ones of the world, then I maim your soul and distance you from Christ. What good is it for you to gain security if you lose your own soul?

Always before me lies the temptation to wrap you in privilege, like a blanket that insulates you from the world. But that kind of protection can only undo you. James Baldwin exhorts his nephew in *The Fire Next Time* to resist self-abnegation. "[Y]ou can only be destroyed by believing that you really are what the white world calls a n——r." Baldwin claims that a person can be destroyed by believing she is less than human, so he writes as a warning but also as a tribute to a black humanity that is not destroyed, that will not be destroyed, despite the terrible forces at work on it. To his insight I add another: you can also be destroyed, daughter, by believing that others are less than human.

As a white girl, you face both temptations: to accept the denial of your humanity and to participate in the denial of others' humanity. All people face these temptations in more and less profound ways, in different ratios and proportions. But you will face a particular paradox—a tension between the whiteness that places you on the side of the powerful and the femaleness that places you on the side of the less powerful. As white, you will find a world of privilege ready to blind you to the violent realities of racism in our world. As female, you will meet people who will try to reduce you to your body, your body to your sexuality, your sexuality to their desire for you, their desire for you to violence. How will I help you to navigate these reductions? I am not sure I navigate them well myself. Sometimes I believe it gets easier as I get older and learn to inhabit my own skin. Sometimes it seems only to become more complicated. Yesterday, for example.

I was jogging through our neighborhood, and running past a car, I heard a voice shout something to me, some comment on my body, as other voices laughed. Hidden in their car, my harassers remained disembodied voices to me. But the voices crawled under my skin. The comment and the laughter felt like a claim on my body, both aggressive and evaluative. At one time in my life I would have felt embarrassed by the comments, as if I had done something to provoke them. I would have tried to slip by as quietly and quickly as possible, the aggressors' voices determining how we occupied that space together. But time and your life have made me braver about my body. I could almost feel your arms circling my neck from our good-bye a few minutes ago, the pressure of your vulnerable body against mine. As the men cackled, anger rose up in me like heat, and I—theologian, mother, resident of that neighborhood—flipped them off as I continued apace. What can I say, daughter? It was the mode of resistance I found at that instant, my way of refusing to be reduced to the men's violent desire. But it was not a particularly creative or peaceful act of resistance.

Your life will be complicated. You will face people who will try to diminish you, and you will likely be tempted to diminish others. You will have to learn when to say no to suffering and when saying no to suffering is really a way of saying no to love or joy. You began discerning this lesson when you decided to seek the joy of other plays knowing you would suffer the pain of their conclusion. As you grow, the dilemmas will become more difficult, and the mystery of suffering—of when to suffer for love and when love requires saying no to suffering—is one you will live with over the course of your life.

Christians' attempts to navigate suffering well have been fraught. Almost since Christianity's beginning, people have invoked its teachings to reconcile the less powerful ones of the world to lives of violence and exploitation. How do we discern the love willing to risk death from the love of death itself? In his book *Between the World and Me*, styled as letter to his son, Ta-Nehisi Coates describes his unease with images of black Civil Rights activists suffering in their nonviolent resistance. He mentions films in which "the black people ... seem to love the worst things in life—love the dogs that rent their children apart, the tear gas that clawed at their lungs, the firehoses that tore off their clothes and tumbled them into the streets." His suspicion is directed toward the white institutions that showed him these films as a school child ("Why are they showing this to us?"), but there is the question of what the activists are doing as well. The image of black activists throwing their bodies to dogs stays with me. Is this nonviolent resistance underwritten by the kind of self-abnegation Baldwin warns against?

I share Coates's suspicion of the way the Civil Rights Movement is edited and presented to the young, though I don't share his interpretation of the activists themselves. I see the cross of Christ in these Civil Rights activists, the love that risks suffering, not the love of suffering itself. I see the love born from the hope of a different world—not the hope to escape to a different world but the hope that this world might be different. I see the Civil Rights activists as loving the world the way Christ did, helping redeem its better nature. But at the same time, I feel the weight of Coates's worry. Saying yes to suffering can be a way of strengthening the death-dealing forces at work in the world. On the other hand, saying no can be a way of keeping suffering ones at bay, of wrapping yourself in privilege and shutting out the reality of the world. Saying no to suffering, in other words, can also strengthen death-dealing forces. It can be difficult to distinguish the love that fears no suffering from the love of suffering itself. At times, Christianity looks suspiciously close to necrophilia.

The question of suffering has also been central to feminist theology. Feminist theology was born from the insight that the traditional narrative of sin and redemption does not speak to the situation of many women—not, at least, in liberatory ways. Theologies that emphasize pride as the cardinal sin and self-sacrificial love as the redemptive path pretend a false universality, feminists have pointed out. Women in a patriarchal world are often too quick to give themselves up, too prone to suffer abuse, too ready to withdraw. The traditional descriptions of sin and redemption thus not only fail to address women's situation; they can also maintain women's oppression. And isn't this the clichéd fate of so many women, especially mothers—to sacrifice themselves, their interests, their talents, their needs, for those around them? With this insight, feminist theology began to take shape, attending to the lives of women as sources for theological reflection.

In the first wave of feminist theology, feminist theologians claimed that the cardinal sin of women in a patriarchal world was not so much the denial of suffering. It was suffering's ready embrace, an embrace often seen as imitating Christ. Feminist theologians wanted to deny that suffering abuse was the way of true discipleship of a God who suffered the cross. They wanted to emphasize Jesus as divine wisdom (the feminine Sophia), as a liberator of women, and as the kingdom of justice and equality. But the agenda of these early feminists, too, pretended a false universality.

For the most part, the first women recognized as feminist theologians were white; over the years, women of color gained voices in the conversation. When white feminist theologians minimized Christ's suffering on the cross, womanist and black feminist theologians pointed out the problem in this approach. White feminists' dismissal of the suffering Christ seems to reproduce white women's refusal to come to terms with the suffering of black women and their complicity in it. There is a long history of enslaved black women who found comfort in the image of Jesus suffering, like them, at the hands of an oppressive regime. One of the most famous early womanist theologians, Delores Williams challenged the idea that suffering is intrinsically redemptive and dismissed the way the cross has been glorified as a model of suffering for all to embrace. At the same time, Williams insisted on the importance of Christ's suffering on the cross. The cross witnesses to a suffering that speaks powerfully to the lives of many, particularly black women. So to suppress the suffering of the cross, as many white feminists have done, is to suppress an important source of solidarity and hope. Williams's theology exposed the way that feminist theologians who claimed to speak for female experience as such were in fact speaking for the experience of white women. Womanist theologians drew on traditions white women forgot, suppressed, or did not reckon as theological sources—traditions like the slave narratives and the history of black women.

Womanist theologians remembered a Jesus who was told he was less than human. But many also emphasized that Jesus was not defeated by death and suffering. He was not destroyed by those who hated him, those who wrapped themselves in comforting delusions about the world, their power, their invulnerability. And so Jesus is a figure of hope that white supremacy will not have the final say. These womanist theologians had a different way of talking about Christ than the early white feminists did. In claiming to speak for women, white feminists asserted a false sisterhood that ignored the deep differences in women's histories.

Over time, the conversations in feminist theology opened to womanist theology, and then to *mujerista* theology and various Asian women's theology and across more and different identities as the diversity of this conversation began to reflect the diversity of women's lives in our world. It turns out that the suffering of Jesus plays differently in different women's lives, for suffering is multivalent, its meanings marshaled toward different political and theological projects.

Christ's suffering can be claimed for either liberating or oppressive ends. Suffering itself can be the way of love or the denial of love. How do I say no to both the patriarchy that wants you to see a degraded version of yourself and the white supremacy that tempts you to see a degraded version of others? And how do I, in my life with you, say no to fetishizing or denying suffering? So much of my maternal sin comes from a warped desire to dominate you in destructive and death-dealing ways; but what of my other impulse, to suffer for you and protect you from suffering?

At one point in the *Confessions*, Augustine laments his own love as too prone to suffering. He has plunged into despair at the death of his friend. He becomes so lost in it that he describes himself as becoming a great question to himself. "How stupid man is to be unable to restrain feelings in suffering the human lot! . . . So I boiled with anger, sighed, wept, and . . . carried my lacerated and bloody soul." Love has taken him into suffering, but his suffering is diseased. His suffering reveals his disordered way of loving, the way of loving another human as if he is eternal, as if a person can pour herself into another and find herself secured by that other. This is a wrong way to love, for Augustine. It is a way of loving in which the self dissipates, diffused into problems, questions, and pain.

But the alternative to such self-undoing grief is not waspish repression and defensiveness. It is not to resist giving oneself in love to a beloved. That, too, is a way of trying to secure oneself that will ultimately fail, leaving the self more fragile than ever. A person has to find a way of giving herself in love without giving away her selfhood. To resist giving herself at all is an attempt to avoid dissipation by opting for a kind of domination, and it is doomed to failure. Domination and dissipation come together, as sins that cannot be separated. I see that there is domination, at least, in my own dissipation, that my attempt to suffer for you is also an attempt to control your life by limiting its exposure. The temptation to save you from suffering can express a lust for domination and yearning for control over what is ultimately un-controllable. The domination of diffusion derives from the illusion that I can absorb the world for you and so by my love create for you a painless world. "What madness," as Augustine writes, "not to understand how to love a human being with awareness of the human condition!"

The way you love a human being, daughter, is the way Christ loves her: all the way through suffering. For Christ suffers, not to eradicate the possibility of our suffering here and now, but to show us the way suffering accompanies love in this world, and the way love survives such suffering *as* love, rather than turning into violence. My attempts to give too much to you, to take away your pain, or to absorb the suffering of the world so that you will not see it—these can be attempts at playing God in a way that God does not even play God. God does not clear the world of suffering for us. God wants us to survive suffering without being defeated by it; this is what I want to help you do, too.

For women, as for all of us, agency and empowerment come not in denying suffering, nor in embracing it, but in a hope that risks devastation, in a nearness to suffering that is funded by faith that suffering is not the final word. The cross extends a hope that is so near despair because it is willing to pass through the possibility of despair. To suffer the way of love is to be willing to suffer, and to suffer the way of love as a parent is also to be willing to let you suffer. I think of Moses's mother, who, after hearing that the Pharaoh wanted to kill all boys under two, fashioned a basket for her son and sent him down the stream to Pharaoh's daughter. It is an act of hope that seems, like the cross, so near despair. Can I imagine putting you in a basket and sending you across the river, on the possibility that a stranger would have mercy on you and draw you from the water? Can I imagine saying good-bye to you forever, giving up all influence on your life, because I wanted you to live? This hope that you were floating toward life could not be prized away from the melancholy realization that life with me would be short, that you were not safe in my home. Moses's mother must be one of the most courageous people in Scripture. Her love was so strong, so unsentimental, so creative. How did she prepare herself to suffer that uncertainty, to suffer the possibility of her child's suffering and death?

This image of a mother sending baby Moses in a basket on the river takes me to another mother, another babe in a river, and an open casket. Many know the story of Emmett Till. He was a fourteen-year-old boy when a white woman said he verbally assaulted and grabbed her in a grocery store, setting off a series of events in which he was beaten, shot, and drowned in a river. When his body was recovered, his face was unrecognizable, his body identified by a ring his mother had given him. After an hour deliberating, his killers were acquitted by an all-white, all-male jury; years later, the woman accusing him admitted she had lied. His mother insisted on an open casket funeral. Rankine reports the mother's words, "Let the people see what I see. I believe that the whole United States is mourning with me." Her faith that the terrible image of her son's mutilated body could invite people into the mourning of black life strikes me as another gesture of maternal hope that is so very near despair. And given the role the image played in galvanizing the Civil Rights Movement, perhaps her hope was vindicated. Given the history of violence against black bodies throughout and since that movement, perhaps not.

How can a person enter the suffering of another? How can you and I enter the mourning of black life? How can we share the vulnerability experienced by women and girls?

In preparation for the memorial march and service here in Waco, I have been reading with my students W.E.B. Du Bois's short story inspired by the lynching, "Jesus Christ in Texas." The story is set in Waco and was circulated after the lynching, along with the souvenir photographs of Jesse Washington's charred body, as part of an anti-lynching campaign. Mulling over the tale, I am struck by one particular similarity to Emmett Till's: a white woman's vulnerability serves as the pretext for attacking a black man. How much violence is inflicted in attempts to secure what seems vulnerable? How much suffering is caused in efforts to avoid suffering? Or at least, how often is avoiding suffering the justification for inflicting the same?

We decide to attend the memorial march as a family. You and a friend carry a sign I made. It says, "We remember Jesse Washington." It is March and still cold in the early morning, but you are warmed by your own exuberance. You see the reporters and feel that we are part of something big and important. When we arrive at the courthouse, we sing "We Shall Overcome." You like the singing, and as soon as it ends, you announce you are ready to eat lunch. Soon you are whining. A meltdown seems imminent. As I plot our path to food, I tamp down frustration at your quick leap from this numinous, intense march to your desire for a sandwich. Have you felt the gravity of what we are marching for? You are a child, I know, and I cannot, I remind myself, expect a march to connect you to the racial horrors in our midst. We live in a world that denies the reality of the suffering ones all around us. It will take more than a march and a story to break through our collective fantasy.

The next year we go to another march, one for women, and this time I invite you to write your own sign. I go through several possible slogans with you, and you rework them until you at last settle on your own: "Only love, not fear." You ask your aunt to write it, and together we set out on the slow-moving march winding its way through the downtown streets of Austin. It is much longer than the march we did together last year, and by the end, you are bored, hungry, and thirsty. I ask you what you liked most about the march—the clever signs we saw, the big, buzzy energy all around us, the way people can come together to make change? You liked the older woman giving out cupcakes to marchers in celebration of her birthday.

Who could blame you? Cupcakes are so concrete and delicious, while the commitments motivating the march are remote to you. Taking you into the reality of suffering will be hard work. As long as suffering is an abstraction, how can anyone enter it? Emmett Till's mother knew that when she opened the casket to reveal the suffering of her son. The NAACP knew that when it published the photographs of Jesse Washington. And so did W.E.B. Du Bois when he circulated his short story. Fantasies of security and peace cannot be dispelled by abstractions.

That means your father and I have to consider how to open our lives more to the vulnerable ones of the world. And it means I cannot ask you to enter the suffering of another by denying or minimizing your own suffering. Without your own experiences of pain, how can you know another's? Others' pain will remain out of reach unless you can connect them to what you know of suffering. Maybe the experience of losing your own community at theater camp can help you fathom the losses of others. And if you learn to see your own suffering as a way of drawing near to the suffering of others, then perhaps the vulnerability of your female body in a patriarchal world can take you nearer to black flesh and its precarious existence in America today. Maybe the experience of theater camp—the joy it gave you and the pain of its loss—can help you learn that to shield yourself from the world's pain is also to shield yourself from all its joy and love. Maybe it can also teach me to check my impulses to sequester you from suffering and so inspire me to seek new and more substantial forms of solidarity, with *Our Lady Mother of Ferguson* and with all mothers mourning their children. Maybe our own particular pain can take us into the larger pain of the world.

To love one another is to risk suffering for that love. With love comes the possibility of loss, nearness to the miserable, and the acknowledgment of separateness. It is not just that mercy involves suffering. All love does—at least it does in this world. My love wants to protect you from suffering, but my love means I must learn to let you suffer. To attempt to eradicate pain from your life would damage you more than pain itself could. What madness not to understand how to love a human being with awareness of the human condition.

I have no key that can unlock the mystery of suffering, no clear formula for distinguishing pathological suffering from the suffering that shows a healthy heart in a world of loss. I see that suffering must never serve as its own end. It must be ordered to love. Suffering may emerge from faithfulness to the way of love and avoiding the siren song of security. But love also means saying no to suffering, when the pain of a relationship signals not new growth but abuse. I want you to learn that way of love, of saying love's yeses and noes, and I hope to learn it better with you. Love, after all, can be convincingly mimicked by what betrays it. My discernment of love must be constantly renewed, so that I do not betray you in suffering, either by denying or embracing it.

CHAPTER 5

Desire

Where was I when I was seeking for you? You were there before me, but I had departed from myself. I could not even find myself, much less you.

Zadie Smith, Anthony Trollope, and Elena Ferrante sit in a sad little pile on the floor, edged off my nightstand by an ever-growing stack of books on motherhood—not the motherhood books that tell me how to care for you (though I read plenty of those while pregnant), but the ones that narrate a woman's becoming a mother. In my own motherhood, I have become strange to myself, and I want some explanation for it, or at least some company in my alienation. Reading Rachel Cusk, I discover the line, "Birth . . . divides women from themselves." And also, "I am surprised to discover how easily I have split in two."

Cusk has named a profound source of my strangeness: to become a mother is to be reborn as a divided self. Motherhood is the movement of one body becoming two, one life becoming two, and the mother is called to both lives, not to effect their unity but to aid their separation. I find myself pulled both to my life and to yours—pulled, as ever, to my talents, interests, and possibilities that extend beyond you; yet always I am drawn to you, called to you at every moment. There is never a time when I hand off my motherhood, even if I temporarily hand over your care. You are my charge—mine and your father's. And still your life does not exhaust my own.

What am I to do with these two ways of being, the new way of motherhood and the old way of my former-and-still-present self? They coexist sometimes well, sometimes uneasily. On my worst days, I remain caught between these two modes, toggling back and forth without fully inhabiting either. Caring for you, I am distracted by my classes and projects and work. Once in my office, I fret about your well-being. Where can I be whole again? If in motherhood I have been born again as a divided self, what kind of rebirth can restore me to wholeness?

This morning, I am preparing for class. Today we are reading the climactic chapters of Augustine's *Confessions*, when Augustine prays to God in the garden of Milan. It is one of my favorite sections of his book, as Augustine contemplates story after story of lives rupturing and transforming in response to God's call and by his example nudges the reader toward her own self-examination. They are nested baskets of conversion stories, with one inside another inside another, and all of these stories woven into Augustine's own conversion. They build toward it in high emotional drama. It usually provokes my students' liveliest discussions, as we wonder together about when Augustine's conversion begins.

The most generative conversion story in the book is Antony's, whose narrative yields a harvest of conversions in the *Confessions* and ultimately bears fruit in Augustine's own life. Antony's pivotal moment occurs when he is already a Christian, after his parents have died. He is in church one day when the Scripture reading rivets him. It is the words of Jesus to the rich young ruler—*Go, sell all you have, and give it to the poor*—but Antony hears them as God's words spoken directly to him. Setting aside money for his sister, Antony obeys, divesting himself of his parents' wealth and beginning a monastic life.

Long after Antony's life, his conversion continues to inspire others to make similar conversions. Augustine recounts the story of a man reading about Antony, who then converts to the celibate life and tells his friend about it, who also converts. Soon they tell their fiancées, who likewise convert. Clearly it is a potent story, and Augustine ponders it over the course of the book, while agonizing over his own failure to lay hold of the life he admires. Lamenting the lust that holds him back, Augustine is divided against himself.

Along with the conversion stories it inspires, Antony's tale becomes a mirror to Augustine's soul, revealing to him his own ugliness. He is trapped in habits he does not want, desiring what he does not want to desire, doing what he hates. Disgusted, exhausted, wretched, he flings himself to the ground under a fig tree, as he weeps to the Lord. *How long, oh Lord?* Like Christ, he prays his misery with the Psalms.

Augustine's agony is interrupted by the voice of a child, who repeats, over and over again, as if in a game, "*Tolle lege, tolle lege.*" Take and read, take and read. At that moment, Augustine remembers Antony's conversion. When Antony heard the gospel reading at church, he received the words as his own call to conversion. If Antony was converted by the words of Scripture, why not Augustine? Augustine hurries over to the Bible, opens it, and reads the first passage he comes across: "Not in riots and drunken parties, not in eroticism and indecencies, not in strife and rivalry, but put on the Lord Jesus Christ and make no provision for the flesh in its lusts." Streams of relief flow through Augustine, washing away all doubt and inconstancy "at once." He has found peace. He is converted, reborn.

They are stern words, these verses that occasion Augustine's conversion—stern and familiar; doubtless Augustine had read them before. But the child's voice gives him these words as a new grace. Heard through the story of Antony, the child's voice signals to Augustine he will be given words for abundant life, and when the verses he finds in Scripture speak to his struggle with lust, he joyfully receives them as words of healing. The words become for Augustine a gift that severs him from his rebellious impulses and restores his will to oneness. I prepare my notes for my students, reading again this account that has enthralled Western Christians for more than 1,500 years. I write down potential discussion questions. What about Augustine, precisely, is converted at this moment? In what ways is this conversion singular, and in what ways is it one among several conversions Augustine undergoes? In particular, how is the transformation in Book VIII different from the one in Book V?

I admire Augustine, the way he receives this grace of an undivided self by finally giving himself to God. I admire him—and I envy him. Motherhood has made me a divided self in a different way, an unhealable way. I yearn for you. I feel the pull of my work. Though the rhythm of my two vocations as mother and professor can be generative, I also feel the competing tugs of each. My two wills and two selves are doomed, it seems, to twoness. My mind drifts, and I imagine my own *tolle lege* moment, in which I open the Bible in great hope and anticipation, and then land on John 3:4, "How can anyone be born after having grown old? Can one enter a second time into the mother's womb and be born?" No, Nicodemus, there is no re-entry to the mother's womb, and there is no climactic resolution for this kind of divided will.

My struggle is both continual and intermittent, the resolution of one episode undone in the dilemma of the next. Any self-unity is temporary and dubious. Always I am vulnerable to accusations of failed responsibilities, shoddy labor, and shallow love—from myself or you or colleagues or friends or family. Augustine is riven by a moral dilemma neatly contained by the movements of his own frayed will; I am riven by social expectations, both internalized and externally reiterated. Writing about her entrance into academic work, one woman expresses her own riven life, "It is peaceful. I am grateful. I am lost. My children are not with me."

I, too, am grateful for my work. I find meaning and purpose in it; it makes my life richer. And still I miss you when we are apart, and I am missing parts of your life to do my work. Your life has given me happiness, depth, and beauty, and when I work, I close you out, often literally. Now it is Saturday morning, and I have left you to eat pancakes with your father while I enclose myself in my study, shutting the door behind me. I feel fated to constant loss, like a person who has lived in two very different countries she loves. Can both parts of me ever feel satisfied?

Part of the difficulty of our twoness is simply your separateness from me; we want and need different things. And part of it is how endless your needs and desires seem right now, which means there is no reprieve from my role of caregiver in this season of life. Then there is a third part of the difficulty: how very divergent our desires are. Though Maria Montessori describes the child and the adult as two poles of humanity, I sometimes feel like we are two different universes. Your universe is organized by play, which is, as one psychologist puts it, "the signature of childhood." Play is your work. By play you grow and change and explore the world. But I often find entering into your spirit of play more difficult than meeting your needs. I don't think it is just the time pressures that make playing difficult for me. It is also difficult because often (forgive me, daughter) I find your play boring. What is this, my resistance to play, my difficulty entering into its spirit?

It is not that play is always a challenge for me. Sometimes I'm swept into your silliness and fun. Sometimes when we're playing, I see your imagination at work, and it fills me with happiness and wonder. You invent ice-cream cat, combining your two great loves into a cat head with an ice cream cone body. You tell stories wild enough to mystify a surrealist. You turn our living room into a fort, our doorway into a stage, our couch into a magical unicorn we ride all over your imagined world.

Even when you were an infant, you loved to play. I would pretend to gobble you up, and you would giggle and squeal as I played at biting your belly. Already you knew the difference between a true threat and pretend. Well before you could talk, you would imitate sounds that I made, and when I caught a little glint in your eye as you did, I would imitate you right back. We would go back and forth and back and forth until the game collapsed into laughter. (Then, of course, I was sated with play, while you were ready for the next round and the next and the next.)

We went to El Salvador when you were small, and there you spoke the universal language of play with the children. You did not need much verbal language to play tag, kick a ball, or pretend to be animals. Play, this pre- or extraverbal mode of communication, imparted to you all the Spanish you needed. Soon you were teaching me that *pato-pato-ganso* is duck-duck-goose. You and the Salvadorans your age bonded as children, as those who love to play. Even I, with my meager Spanish, could bond with the children in ways I could not, absent interpretation, with the adults. With your new Salvadoran friends, we played the animal game, where one of us would call out an animal and the rest would have to move across the floor in the spirit of that creature. We all communicated easily, and I never wondered how ridiculous I looked imitating the gait of elephants, giraffes, frogs, and kitty cats.

Sometimes you and your play-lovingness open up new worlds of possibility for who I can be and suggest a different sociality, not just for me but for our world. When you were very small, we used to play peekaboo in the grocery cart; now we often play "I spy." People, by and large, smile indulgently at us as they pass us by in their more mission-driven carts. I can't help but think about how they might look at me if you weren't here, and I were acting this silly on my own. I realize that you give me an excuse to be silly in public. It would be difficult for me enjoy such silliness without you.

Maybe this is why, in Scripture, David is so beloved of God. David is willing to be silly, dancing in his linen ephod "with all his might" as he celebrates the return of the Lord's presence with the ark of the covenant. His poor wife Michal is disgusted by his lack of decorum. She is the adult in this scenario; David is the child. She lives out the rest of her life childless, an implied divine judgment on her disgust at David's childlikeness.

What is it that makes me more like Michal than like David? Of course, I need to think about adult things some of the time. We cannot all of us be dancing fools always or the human race would starve. It is good to have two different poles of humanity, one ordered to play and the other to purpose. There is something important and worthy about our difference from one another. But I think there are other sides to our difference as well. I resist play in part because of my own materialism. I contain your wild energy so that you don't break my objects or tear my clothes or soil our furniture. How many times have I heard myself saying to be careful not to damage some object? What am I teaching you with these constant lessons about the importance of material goods?

My materialism compounds another anti-play tendency. I have difficulty pursuing something without an explicit goal. I constantly look to objectives, measures, and function, even in most of my weekend activities. I clean, run errands, cook, make headway on my to-do list. Play, on the other hand, is not functional. It has that in common with religion. The activities of play and religion are not reducible to a need or function; but neither are they pointless.

One time when you were younger and in play-therapy, we had an appointment on a day when you had managed to successfully negotiate a toilet situation that had been causing you anxiety for months. Normally in therapy your anxieties rooted you to the floor, and you sat mute and frozen. But on this day, you walked in purposefully, went to the sandbox, and scanned the dozens of little toys to find a large toilet, which you lifted up and set in the sandbox. For the next several minutes, you poured sand on the toilet, covering it and uncovering it, filling it with sand and rediscovering it, as your therapist and I stood by silently. It seemed to me that in this play, you were performing a ritual of mastery, celebrating and claiming your victory.

By play, you create your own world, transposing experiences into a new world. It is how you create a symbolic world and make meaning from life. It was for you on that day in therapy how you were incorporating the toilet into a new place in your reality, how you moved from avoidance to encounter and also how you expressed that move. By play, you were coming to find your place in the world.

In fact, play is how humans have found their place in the world over the millennia. Play is what gives birth to much of human culture: storytelling, meaning-making, art, ritual, and religion. Through play we learn to be human. Through play we learn to worship.

Romano Guardini probes this connection between play and ritual in his book on the Roman Catholic liturgy. A contemporary of fellow Catholic Maria Montessori, whose work he knew,

Guardini describes the playfulness of Mass as a puzzle or irritation for some. Why is the liturgy so elaborate and meandering, when the sacrifice of the Mass could be achieved directly in a few simple words? Why such superfluous standing, sitting, crossing, repeating, and singing—taking an hour for what might take a few moments? None of these are necessary for the central sacrifice. But the purposelessness of the liturgy helps us lay hold, for Guardini, of the abundant life. Sounding like Montessori, he writes, "The child, when it plays, does not aim at anything. It has no purpose. It does not want to do anything but to exercise its youthful powers, pour forth its life in an aimless series of movements, words and actions, and by this to develop and to realize itself more fully; all of which is purposeless, but full of meaning nevertheless." He then explains, "That is what play means; it is life, pouring itself forth without an aim, seizing upon riches from its own abundant store, significant through the fact of its existence." For Guardini, worship is a type of deeply committed play. Following Guardini's thought decades later, the then-future Pope Benedict XVI wrote that liturgy should be "the rediscovering within us of true childhood, of openness to a greatness still to come, which is still unfulfilled in adult life." The child at play is an image for the kind of openness to life that adults should cultivate—that, in fact, the liturgy is trying to help people discover. In church I am seeking my true childhood.

Later that evening, after play therapy, I go with you and your father to church, for the Vigil Mass. I try to the think about the Pope's words as you fidget through the service, inventing games that others find distracting. Often during these moments, irritation mounts in me as I snap at you to close your eyes for prayer, stand up for the gospel, and recite the prayers you know. Have I found ways of reducing even worship to a series of goals? I know that, in my impatience, I'm not imparting to you a disposition of prayer. Sometimes I think we adults find ways to drain the joy and play out of even those places where they should bubble forth most freely. I, at any rate, seem to move in that direction. Today I pray for the grace to enter into the spirit of true childhood your playfulness points to. By the end of Mass, I am, at least, less frustrated than usual.

The older I get, the more I find myself tempted to close myself to the world. I have learned how things go, how people are. And that knowledge has made me less patient, less prone to wonder, less open to new ideas and ways of being. The openness that was natural to me as a child has to be cultivated in me as an adult. You help with that. Just when I was beginning to settle into my adulthood, you came along and unsettled me. Just when the play of my adolescence and even my twenties was coming to an end, you introduced new sources of it in my life. I am grateful, and I sometimes resent it. I am David; I am Michal.

But it is not really a fair comparison, after all, between David and Michal. I imagine David's childlike exuberance was something the world of ancient Mesopotamia worked to stamp out of women. Could Michal find and express a joy that flouted social decorum? If, by some miracle, she had managed to nurture a desire that coursed through her in an uninhibited dance of adoration, would that spectacle of female desire, joy, and vitality be celebrated as David's was? Or would it be punished as transgression?

Even from my own very different life as a woman in late modernity, I suffer estrangement from my own desires. They slip away from me, melting into your need, someone's agenda, my own compulsions, the machinery of the world. I am surprised how easily I cede my desires. At one level, the problem is simply the number of obligations I have—to you, your father, my undergraduates, my graduate students, my colleagues, my family, my friends. As a journalist recently wrote, "A woman retains so many obligations to so many people that she must, almost always, strip-mine her selfhood to achieve ... success and security." True, and yet the problem of my dissipating desires is not just the way my obligations overtake them. Even in those activities that first inspired me to academic life—my writing and research—I allow my desires to be eroded by a sea of expectations. An essay I wanted to write becomes a deadline an editor wants me to meet. A speaking opportunity becomes an occasion for pleasing my host. An event I enthusiastically envisioned becomes one more project I promised to another set of people. Material security replaces the pleasures of learning, doing, and growing. I allow my desires to be worn away by the drive to please, to succeed, to meet the hopes of others. I am tempted to replace the Socratic injunction to know thyself with the more pragmatic advice to know the expectations, desires, and needs of those surrounding thyself.

Why do I wander away from my own desires? It must be in part that I don't want to be selfish—that deadly sin all mothers are judged against. Still, I don't think that gets to the bottom of my problem. I wonder if I'm afraid of my desires—afraid, I mean, that I can't fulfill them or that they won't fulfill me. What if I allow myself to be guided by my desires, and a desire fizzles out and leaves me lost in a dark wood? What if I'm wrong about my desires, or have no idea how to meet them? What if they leave me exposed to the world? It is easier and more straightforward to fulfill the expectations of others and meet social standards than attempt the more nebulous task of discerning and satisfying my own longings. I can see that I am on the right path—or at least *a* path—when I fulfill commitments and please people.

This is a problem with me, and it is a problem larger than me. The problem of female desire has lately been in the news—specifically, female sexual desire, as communities attempt to reckon with our present culture of sexual assault. In one article, a woman who had just written a book about consent describes an interview with a young female reporter. After the official interview, the reporter asks, "How do you know what you want to say 'yes' or 'no' to in bed?" The author claims this exchange captures one of many times women voiced alienation from their desires to her. Another female writer wrestling through the depth of the sexual assault crisis describes in an article the way many women tolerate pain as a normal part of their sexual experience. "Women," she writes, "are enculturated to be uncomfortable most of the time. And to ignore their discomfort." She points to gender bias in sex research—there are five times more studies on erectile dysfunction (men's pleasure) than on dyspareunia (women's severe pain during sex)—as evidence for how little society values women's pleasure and pain. And women are socialized into this system from a young age. They're complimented primarily for their prettiness as young girls and so learn to take their pleasure vicariously. "At every turn," she writes, "women are taught that *how someone reacts to them* does more to establish their goodness and worth than *anything they themselves might feel.*" Having learned to outsource their pleasure to third parties, women can all too easily become poor interpreters of their desire.

Yet. If God is the one in whom all desires are satisfied, the one who is Love itself, then how can I find God and ignore my own loves and desires? If I've departed from myself and my loves, how can I find the Love who is already present to me? If I can't find myself, how can I find God? These are Augustine's questions, as his self, his true desire, dissipates in a lust that drives his life and drains him of delight. His problem, perhaps, is the opposite of many women's. He can all too easily discern and pursue his sexual pleasure, but such pursuit has blinded him from his life's deep desires. Pursuing lust, he loses touch with the more difficult work of pursuing love. Estranged from the way of love, he is alienated from both God and himself.

For different reasons, the difficulty of being present to myself and so to God are my problems, too. But you are so mysteriously unlike me in this way. I watch you in your play express an immediacy to your own desires. You take a reflexive delight in the world, and at times, I feel your presence calling me to share in that delight. You want to play the same thing again, again, again. You carry a heavy bag, maximizing your effort lugging it up the stairs; I, of course, would try to minimize effort. Your play is not ordered toward an external goal; it is ordered toward your *becoming*. In a way, then, your play, though arising from delight, is ordered to my work. Your play prepares you to be an adult and do the work adults do; it is playing at adulthood without the consequences of adult choices. But in that ordering, your play is entirely different from my work. Your play is liberated from the measure of external functions. In your play, there is freedom, there is care for the self, there is preparation for the soul to stretch out into the world and toward the divine. Your play reminds me of who I am, how to desire, and what it means to be human. In that way, my work is ordered to your play.

Sometimes, watching you, I fantasize about chucking my job, staying home with you, and playing all the time. Maybe we would move to an island without clocks, schedules, or demands. Instead of teaching university students, I would teach you, my sole pupil. We would rise with the sun, keep our own rhythms, and play all day, living on a little island of delight, where I would never harass you to put on socks and shoes. We would turn our backs to the global economy that parcels and tracks time like a tradeable commodity. It would be marvelous.

At least, it is marvelous in my imagination. In reality, could I bear to live on that island? Can any adult be wholly oriented toward play? Should she? Probably the orientation to work would creep back in. One of us would have to make meals, clean up, and tend needs. Teaching you would become work; and there would be play-dough to pick off the ground and paint to wash off of skin and walls. In the real, nonfantasy world, play and work often come to us intermingled. At times, my academic work seems to me like play—reading, enjoying, growing from texts. But it's amazing how easily that enjoyment can get coopted by other ends—seeking tenure, building my reputation, pursuing financial gain. What was once an end in itself, part of my self's *becoming*, becomes functionalized toward external goals. And it can happen the other way, too, where work can become an occasion for play. I think of those who infuse play into their work by leavening rote physical activities with song, of hair stylists who use their work time to connect with clients, or of designers who approach their work as a primarily artistic endeavor.

I am turning these mysteries of us—our twoness, my work, your play—over and over because they are the realities that leave me sometimes feeling wounded in the world. The wounding, as I experience it, is the curse of a divided self. It is the way I am called to a twoness that never dissolves and desires that frequently do. But is the wounding also a blessing? Can the way I am called to you, can the intransigence of my role as mother, also call me to resist a creeping functionalism? You call me away from work I love, but you also call me away from the financialization of the world, away from the totalizing logic of power and money. In some ways, my wound of division speaks to a deep woundedness in our world that has given itself over too wholly to the logic of markets and capital and monetized time.

I can give into the distortions of the world, treating you as a project, or as a subject-in-making for the empire of global capitalism. I can try to assimilate your play to my functionality, turn all of your toys into objects that make you grow smarter and more talented, or will distract you so that I can work. I can make my logic of work an all-encompassing logic that governs your world. Or I can try to yield to your way of play, let it transform my work and reconnect me to a self that exceeds any function or goal.

I like this idea of transformation, but it is difficult to practice. It is difficult, in part, because I am already colonized by the logics of materialism, functionalism, and capitalism, and because opening myself to another way of being is painful. And it is difficult because I still have to assess at each moment what calling to pursue—whether at this moment here and now I should write theology or nurture your soul. Both of those are good callings, worthy of time and effort. It is not those callings that need to be converted—as if in giving up being a professor, I would find myself closer to God. The conversion is much more complex. It speaks to the transformation of an underlying condition of graspingness, possessiveness, and functionalism, and though being a professor may be more easily assimilated to the untransformed condition than motherhood is, it is not identical with that condition. Then, even when these two vocations are transformed, they remain as two. So I have no climactic moment of visible, identifiable wholeness to reach for. I have only the episodic negotiations of my divided self.

It is Monday now, and I feel the twoness sharply today. You are sick. I am trying to move meetings, reconfigure the day with your father, and squeeze class preparation into the moments you sleep or watch TV. I am not sure I can finish my student's recommendation letter due this afternoon; I am afraid I will miss the faculty vote my colleagues are counting on me to make. My day was overstuffed, and I am forced to face my limitations of time and energy.

You have been watching Netflix the last hour, and you're growing restless. You've begun calling for water that you do not want and asking for help you do not need. I know that you want to feel doted on and cared for, but I am already feeling overextended—spilt dry, as Augustine might say. Reading the *Confessions*, preparing for class, whelmed by a sense of my own failures to others, I recognize the feeling of being strip-mined and lost. I want, like Augustine, my own will called into wholeness.

But how can this desire for wholeness be anything but naïve? In this life, I know, there is no resolution to these competing demands on my self, no way to foreclose a construal of my life as failing these claims. This is modern womanhood: women have wonderful, new opportunities but are still tethered to old expectations. There is no voice, no personal call that can heal me from such rivenness.

You are tugging at me. You've been trying to get my attention for some time now, and you're looking less pitiful. "Mommy, come and play with me!" you whine. "Come and play!" You smile and cock your head, the way you do when you're wheedling me for something. My first thought is that you are better now, and I begin to mentally replan my day. Could I take you to campus for my faculty vote? But you persist. "Come and play!" You are batting your eyes and twisting your mouth into a cartoonish expression of pleading. I cannot help smiling at your theatrics.

There is no voice that can heal me from my rivenness, but your joy, your goofiness, your delight at your own antics, embolden a shy desire. "Come and play!" I remember the child's voice in Augustine and take yours as divine command. Shutting my computer, I swoop you into a hug, dipping you upside down as you break into surprised giggles, exclaiming, "Spin me, Mommy!" I'm giggling now, too. You wiggle to the floor and catch my hand, and the two of us twirl around the room, swinging, hopping, twisting, and dancing with silliness to make even King David blush.

CHAPTER 6

Temptation

As soon as he saw blood, he at once drank in savagery and did not turn away. His eyes were riveted. He imbibed madness. Without any awareness of what was happening to him, he found delight in the murderous contest and was inebriated by bloodthirsty pleasure.

Your hands are not clasped. You are not kneeling, nor are your eyes closed. You are rolling around on the floor, staring up at the ceiling and grabbing your feet as we say together, "Our Father, who art in heaven, hallowed be thy name. Thy kingdom come; thy will be done. . . ." Though you are not in the posture of prayer I have tried to teach you—which irritates me—I still love to hear you say the Lord's Prayer, your childish voice lilting up at the end of each line, your recitation emphasizing the rhythm of the words. From your mouth, the prayer sounds like a song.

For several years now, we've been praying the Lord's Prayer together. When you were two, you surprised your father and me one night by declaiming the whole thing outright. I had gotten up to retrieve a calligraphed print of the prayer your godmother gave you, to help you focus during our prayer time, and before I could return to our circle, you started reciting the prayer yourself. I'm sure you had only the dimmest idea what you were saying. But then, I feel like I'm still learning what it means to pray those words.

You have grown older, and I wait for you to ask me about some of the phrases. What does it mean to be delivered from temptation? We've been reading a book, an illustrated version of the prayer, where the pictures tell the story of a girl helping her dad with yard work for an elderly woman. The girl finds a medallion in the yard and is tempted to keep it, but she ultimately returns it to the elderly woman. The woman, who has been fingering an empty chain most of the story, is relieved and grateful to find the medallion that completes her necklace. But after a moment's pause, she gives the medallion to the child, together with the chain for it. On the last page of the book, the medallion is featured in close-up, and the reader sees the Lord's Prayer written on it.

The illustrations interpret a narrative of temptation as central to the Lord's Prayer. The pictures begin, like the prayer itself, by establishing the source of the child's knowledge of goodness—the goodness she can be tempted to stray from. In the pictures' story, the girl's moral sense comes through her earthly father, who figures the girl's heavenly father. Her father is often illumined with light and swirled by white birds that could be doves, even as he is set against a large sky that makes him small by comparison. He signifies a God much bigger than he is. And he reveals the divine to the girl. Her pivotal moment comes when she sees the good way of her father in contrast with her own. He refuses payment from the elderly woman as the daughter grasps the medallion, looking at it uneasily. She realizes now she cannot keep it. Her conscience is shaped by her father's goodness. She knows what it means to pray "thy will be done" because she knows the will of her earthly father.

The story is simple; the resolution of the girl's dilemma seems quick and easy from the perspective of an adult. From the child's view, though, it is painful to assent to "thy will be done" in that scenario. Rather than say it, she initially withdraws her presence from both her father and the woman they are serving. Her eyes glance down. She points her body away. She stops engaging with them, moving to the edge of their conversation. Before she says no to temptation and yes to thy will being done, she absents herself. When she triumphs over temptation, her relationships are renewed; her friendship with the woman deepens. She becomes more present to this little community gathered over yard work.

They are difficult words, "Thy will be done." Whatever our stage in life, uttering them is never easy. At least, they are not easy all the time. Even Jesus struggled as he said them. On the night he is betrayed, Jesus goes out to the garden of Gethsemane to pray. Scripture describes him as sorrowful and agitated. He asks his friends to stay awake with him, for he is "deeply grieved, even to death." Throwing himself on the ground to pray, he begins with words less tranquil than the prayer he gave his disciples. "My Father, if it is possible, let this cup pass from me." His second sentence is similar to that in the Lord's Prayer: "[Y]et not what I want but what you want." Not my will, but thine be done. He prays a second and a third time, repeating both his petition and his consent, asking his Father for reprieve but submitting his will to the Father's. After the third prayer—and the third time he has found his friends sleeping instead of praying with him—he is arrested.

His friends are awake now, tensely observing what happens next. When his betrayer comes, Jesus kisses him and says, "Friend, do what you are here to do." In what follows—as told in Luke and John's gospel especially—Jesus is self-possessed: chastising his arresters, interpreting their actions for them, ordering the various actors about. This, apparently, is what his submitted will looks like: calm, steady, sure. One of his friends, by contrast, chops off the ear of a soldier, nearly bringing trouble upon himself as well as the rest of those gathered. Jesus heals the soldier and rebukes his friend, pointing out that he himself could appeal to his Father for legions of angels if he wanted to win a contest of force. Peter, identified as this friend in the Gospel of John, will go on to deny Jesus three times that night. These wild swings of swords and confidence are, presumably, what a will that chooses mine over thine looks like. It dominates in violence and withdraws in fear, failing to be faithful to the one it wants to love. Peter makes himself absent to Jesus, absent even to himself and his deepest longings, in his willfulness.

What does it mean for us, both of us, to affirm in the midst of temptation, "Not my will but thine?" I take it that you submit your own wants, your proto-will, to your father and me so that you can have a mature will someday. You were born a little bundle of desires, and in the beginning, you expressed all of them. If I were to help you follow all of your desires through early childhood, you would never learn to wholly will something. You would be tyrannized by your own competing wants, unable to enjoy any activity for very long, and so blocked off from the deep pleasures of life like friendship, learning, and literature—all pleasures that also entail deferring or denying desires. In learning to submit your will to mine, you gain the capacity to will something with your whole self; you create a self that can experience deep pleasure. As your parent, I help you learn that integrity and create that self. It is another way that I image for you the divine, like the father in the story of the tempted little girl.

But you who image the Messiah to me, what do you teach me about saying "Not my will but thine"? How and when do I say that to you? As a parent, I sometimes feel my whole life is about yielding to you, your needs, and your desires. Then, there are certain times, especially when I feel your goodness is at stake, that I find myself hardening against you. Prayer time, ironically, is often one such time, when I want you to model what I think attention looks like, but you seem distracted, willful, and silly. I feel a recalcitrant desire to *make* you pray, though I know that impulse is destructive.

There was a time when I could not imagine being angry, really angry, with you. In your first three years of life, you were so malleable and porous. You absorbed the world around you, and my instinct was always to defend and aid you. Even when you woke up multiple times in the night, refused the food I offered, and smeared the contents of your diaper across the floor, I didn't feel anger toward you. I felt exhausted and frustrated, but the kind of hardness I can feel toward you now was foreign to me then. What could I harden myself against? You had no moral sense, no defined center for making and determining action. My frustration was impersonal, for your person was so unformed. You simply wanted or didn't want.

For a similar reason, Aristotle frequently couples children with beasts in his *Ethics*. There is something to that coupling. You once shared a beast's simplicity of desiring. But your simplicity was also different from a beast's. A beast's nature is fairly determined. Yours is radically open, receptive to incarnating the culture, knowledge, distortions, and loves that surround you. Born into the world to be like the world, you are what Maria Montessori calls "an absorbent self." The older you get, the more this radical openness begins to close. Your plasticity begins to stiffen. During this older stage of your absorption, from about three until six years old, your personality takes on a more definitive shape. You have a moral center, even if it is still very much in development. When you turned three, I could begin to teach you explicitly and discipline you. At that point, you often found your moral center by asserting your nascent will—often, it seemed to me, by telling me no and refusing my direction. I learned the term "threenager."

Now there are times—many times—when I run out of patience. I find myself wanting to force you to obey. I feel the ridiculousness of my situation, waiting hand and foot on a tiny creature who knows nothing of what it takes to make the world run, a creature whose every actual need I meet but who throws tantrums when I deny some whim. Sometimes my rage comes quickly, like a storm that blows fiercely in—and suddenly sweeps away. Where does this anger come from? It is unlike any other anger I have experienced, and when something in the situation turns—you look at me wounded or suddenly hug me—I melt, awash in affection and relieved that I did not fully indulge my rage. Sometimes my impatience is subtler, as it usually is when I am coaxing you to say you're sorry.

It is difficult, I think, to teach any child to apologize well, but especially you. You have never said the words "I'm sorry." Sometimes your refusal to say them infuriates me; sometimes it embarrasses me. On occasion, I am tempted to coerce your behavior. All I want, in those moments of temptation, is for you to say the words "I'm sorry." I don't care if you mean them.

This is not the person I want to be, nor you to be. I'm aware of the dangers in teaching you to say words you do not mean to get what you want, to wield your words as instruments of power rather than as media of communication and truth. I think of this—and still in the situation of wanting you to apologize, I find myself in my own arena of great temptation, wanting you to just do it, and I become angrier and more passionate until I am like Augustine's friend Alypius, peering out from his hands at the circus, heaving with desire and dispossessed of himself. Knowing himself excited by the spectacle of violence, Alypius tried to avoid the gladiatorial arena. Once dragged there, he tried to keep himself from temptation by covering his eyes. But as the crowd roared, he looked out from his hands to see the gladiator bloodied by a blow, and he joined the cheer, his soul, in Augustine's narration, felled by a blow still more dangerous.

Alypius is drawn into a spirit of domination by lust of the eyes. I am drawn into the same spirit by a different lust to dominate. How can I resist my temptation? It comes from my desire to help you into the good life—and, less worthily, from my desire to appear to others as if I am doing so. There is some misdirected good in my anger, even as my will is not fully integrated; how can it be healed?

Like Alypius and the gladiator, we have our own double-arena of danger. I enter my arena of temptation when I see you have entered yours. Your battle with pride or fear keeps you from acknowledging your wrong; I battle with watching you struggle. We are like Alypius and the gladiator—but not quite. Alypius is wounded by looking. I am wounded by my inability to simply look. Like a crazed sports fan or confused theatergoer, I am tempted to jump into the arena for you, to replace your decisions with my own, thy will with mine. Both of us, in our arenas, attempt to flee the presence of another; I of you, you of the one you wronged. We are like the little girl who absents herself from her father and the elderly woman in the book illustrating the Lord's Prayer. These two temptations to neglect another (absenting our presence) and to dominate another (enforcing our presence) are two related ways of evading another's presence. To say not thy will but mine is to say, in a way, not you, just me; there is no room for you.

I reflect on Christ's opposite words: *Not my will but thine.* Aren't they dangerous in their own way? Couldn't my submitting to your will be a path toward a different kind of destructiveness, where you never learn to say I'm sorry? Isn't that a more terrible fate than being coerced into socially acceptable behavior? As a parent, I have a responsibility to teach you that your will should not tyrannize all, that it must learn to yield to another. Or do I? Perhaps, as females, neither of us should spend much time rehearsing the line "not my will but thine." The trope of the sacrificial woman—especially the sacrificial mother—is such a cliché. Doesn't my appropriation of "not my will but thine" simply make me one more overly sacrificial woman, abdicating her desires to those of patriarchy? How can I say "not my will but thine" in a patriarchal world without surrendering my selfhood? I don't want either of our lives to be determined by misogyny. But what do I want for us? And how do I rightly pray the words Jesus taught us?

All of this swirls in the back of my brain the night we sit down to watch *Brave*, that Pixar film about a Scottish girl with a mane of curly red hair. Her name is Merida, and like most Disney heroines, Merida is a beautiful young princess destined to marry a prince. Unlike most Disney heroines, she does not want that destiny—not now, at least. She blames her mother for it, and so she decides to change her fate by changing her mother's mind. When persuasion doesn't work, she opts for a magic potion. (It is a sad and familiar irony—which the movie does not satisfactorily explore—that the mother figures patriarchal expectations to her daughter.) Locked in a painful struggle, the mother and daughter both refuse each other's presence. The mother denies the daughter's separateness, intent on bringing her in line with her clan's wishes by dominating her daughter's desires. In doing so, she recreates the scene of her own domination as a young woman, which she has forgotten was once a scene of domination, surrounded as she is now by her happy family and loving marriage. Merida responds to her mother's domination by reciprocating it.

She attempts to force her mother to alter course by magic. But instead of changing her mind, the potion changes her mother into a bear.

Throughout the movie, Merida steadfastly avoids apologizing to her mother-bear for this transformation. Instead, she blames the witch who made the potion. Late in the movie, Merida finally reaches a turning point when she believes the spell is irreversible, faces her mother-bear, and weeps. It is then that she finally apologizes, and the spell is undone. It is a rite of passage, on multiple levels. Merida takes her place in the world by taking responsibility for an outcome she caused—even though she was not wholly responsible for it and certainly did not wish it. In her apology, she assents to her mother's presence, to the claims her mother's life has on her, and to her responsibility of responding to those claims. Her passage to adulthood comes by rite of apology.

I look over at you at this point in the movie. Tears are rolling down your cheeks. You notice my gaze and smile. "Mommy, why are my eyes watering?" you ask. I take you in my lap, and we watch the rest of the movie cuddled together.

Through her apology, Merida claims her place in a fallen world. It is a lesson she learned from her mother the night before. That night, faced with a castle full of anxious suitors and their fathers, Merida had delivered a speech by working off cues from her mother, who (still a bear at this point) signed to her from the shadows. She began by speaking exactly what her mother signed and gradually found a way to improvise. She narrated the history of the clans gathered in the castle in such a way as to identify and claim the flexibility of her role within that history. Her speech gave the people gathered a sense of who they are, of what they have done, and of how their future can make still make sense without requiring her immediately to marry. As the speech goes on, Merida depends less on her mother for her words and ideas, and the monologue becomes more wholly her own. The next day, as she comes to terms with losing her mother permanently, she sees in new horror and sadness her own responsibility for the spell, that her actions have led to this precipice of loss.

I am struck that the structure of Merida's speech to the clans mirrors the logic of apology: acknowledging the past while opening a future that is not determined by that past. Apology, like Merida's mother-inspired speech, is a creative act. The twin temptations for coming of age in a fallen world are to repudiate that world, preferring instead the purity of disengagement, what we might call the innocence of childhood; and to capitulate to it, taking its vices into one's soul so that the world's vices continue on in one's very person. Merida's speech, like an apology, contrasts with both of these. Through apology, she comes of age in a fallen world by claiming responsibility for actions that are both hers and beyond her. She takes on society's vices as her own even while disavowing those vices as the way of the future. For this is Merida's bravery, to resist the twin temptations of fleeing the past and capitulating to it, but instead, like Christ, to bear history into a new age. This is what I want for you: to be brave as Merida is brave, to apologize freely as Merida finally does, to be renewed as Christ renews.

I don't know why you refuse to apologize, but I do know that failure may embody either of the two temptations: fleeing your past and isolating yourself from your community (a claim that you are not responsible), or uncritically merging into them (a claim that there is no sin here to mark). In the case of Merida, both her speech to the clan and her apology to her mother are creative acts of accepting and transforming her history. In finding a new way to stay in her community, she comes to terms with the complexities of her own agency—both the way her agency is shaped by a community and the way she can help shape the community's future. That is what apology does, and that is what I want for you. I want you to learn to apologize even for actions beyond yourself, to come to terms with your agency in a complex and delicate way.

When I attempt to coerce an apology from you, I find myself short-circuiting this complexity. I impart a blunted sense of selfhood. For a coerced apology is a performative contradiction: a community attempting to substitute its own will for the individual's by pressuring an individual to profess responsibility for the community. In the passage from childhood, this responsibility-taking happens (or doesn't), and childhood is that developmental time of learning one's own agency in such a way that one prepares to take this complex place. The apologies you learn to give in childhood model a way of taking your place in the world such that you can enter into a life that is good and virtuous. They model a way of living in community and taking responsibility for the community while also responding to the demands of one's own conscience.

I don't want just to teach to say you the words "I'm sorry." I want to cultivate a disposition of proper sorrow. This word *cultivation* suggests a way of thinking of you that is less like an animal to be mastered and more like a garden to tend. One cannot force a seed to grow. One can only nurture it, encourage it, and prepare the soil. Seeds, like the dispositions and desires of virtue, sometimes do not grow. You are a seed as the kingdom of God is a mustard seed that grows into a magnificent tree, as our present bodies are seeds that die to be raised as resurrection bodies, as Jesus's words are seeds scattered by a sower, some flourishing, some failing to take root, some withering. You are a seed; your growth is both natural and mysterious, under my influence but not my control. You are a seed; I am a gardener. What can I do but lovingly tend to you?

I certainly cannot master you. The control I grasp in coercing you to apologize is ultimately illusory, for you are not a limb of my body. And I don't want you to be a limb. I want you to be your own body, to be the ensouled creature you are. My temptation to rule you is my temptation to deny your strangeness. It is the temptation to dictate your world and prevent you from altering the shape of mine. When I say yes to this temptation, I shield my own will from yours.

How did Jesus learn to say these words of prayer: *Not what I want but what you want,* and *Thy will be done?* They are so difficult. They have to be learned, I think, through a contest with temptation. Perhaps Jesus learned to say them in the beginning of his ministry, which commenced after a time of temptation. In the Gospels of Matthew, Mark, and Luke, after Jesus is baptized, he heads out into the wilderness. While Jesus fasts and prays, a voice of temptation suggests that he turn stones into bread, that he throw himself from the Temple to see if God will save him, and that he worship Satan to receive all the kingdoms of the world. These three temptations all render Jesus as the center of his own existence—his felt needs, his glory, his power take center stage. But Jesus deflects each of them, pointing to the Father's will, the Father's way, the Father's glory. Jesus in this contest claims his vocation as the Image of the invisible God, the one in whom God shines forth. The Son comes to reveal the Father. Christ arrives to show the invisible God. As the Word made flesh, Christ yields fleshly existence to divine life and so teaches us to do the same.

What kind of yielding do you require of me, daughter? When you were a baby, I did everything for you. It was exhausting, but I did things more or less my own way. Now that you are older and assert your own judgment, I confess I do not always like it. In some ways, I want you to be a baby again. I want my own voice to remain sovereign, not to feel the friction of your will against mine.

But you have come into this world, into my world, incarnating the culture and language and humanity around you. You have come into my world as flesh, to help your father and me become children of God. And my transformation requires acknowledging your fleshly existence as separate from my own, your being as beyond my capacity possess it.

The way I oriented my being toward you as a desiring baby has been preparation for this deeper, more painful orientation to you as a willing child. It means learning to say to you: Not my will but thine. I cannot say it absolutely. I cannot say it as a way to end a standoff or to leave you languishing in your own self-tyranny. I say it as my hope, as the end to which I am pressing as a parent. "Not my will but thine" is the state I am working for, when you can live into your freedom to love, and I can submit to that work. Neither coercion nor abandonment moves us toward this hope. I must somehow find a way to stay with you, to abide with you in a way that helps your will grow toward its end of freedom and love.

CHAPTER 7

Domination

What torments my heart suffered in mental pregnancy,
what groans my God!

We are locked in a bathroom in a café. While washing our hands, you had elbowed your friend in the nose, and now you won't apologize for hurting her. It was an accident, you claim; why apologize for an accident? Your friend is upset. Her mother is outside, reserving a table for us. I will not let you out of the bathroom until you apologize; if you refuse, you will lose the pink lemonade we came for.

We have been at this for some minutes now. You have grown more hysterical. You won't apologize. You can't, you insist. You want pink lemonade, you wail. It's not fair, you howl; you didn't mean to hurt her. I wonder if your tortured cries echo through the café. I try not to be swayed by your pitiful moans. I am Lady Justice, deaf and blind with my scales, consoled by my own righteousness. I am a stone statue, unyielding, unmoved, unmerciful.

Yet I can see that my hardness bruises you. I know I'm not helping you toward the good but entrenching you in your own misery. Now, however, my frustration is buttressed by my pride. I am past the point of changing tactics. I will not bend to your bad behavior. Seeing you commit to your own misery only hardens me further. Maddened that you are choosing unhappiness over obedience, I am enveloped by wrath.

Your anger shakes your whole body with its violence, while my icy rage freezes any floes of tenderness that trickle through my heart. As you continue to resist me, I feel my cold fury mounting its own violent force. I ask you again to say, "I'm sorry." Facing me, you counter that you cannot and propose instead to tell your friend that I want you to apologize to her. The absurdity of this non-apology magnifies my rage, and I erupt in moralized lecture.

Going into this confrontation, I had multiple motives. I wanted you to flourish and be good. I wanted you to obey me and make me look like a good mother. But the latter reasons have eclipsed the former ones. All I want is for you to do what I say. *Libido dominandi*, the lust to dominate, possesses me. I have lost sight of your good.

The standoff ends when I, for the first and only time in our relationship, trick you into saying you're sorry. Without blinking my eyes or breaking my gaze, I stare at you for a long moment before saying deliberately and quietly, as if any sound or movement might cause me to explode, "Those are not the words you need to say. What have I asked you to say?" You look at your friend and me, confused by my intensity. "I'm sorry?" Your friend jumps in, "It's okay, I forgive you." Her prompt, prim recital certifies the apology. My rage immediately melts, though you, despite your pink lemonade, are now sulky as you absorb what has just happened. I am jovial and joking with you, attempting to coax you from your poutiness. Victory, however dubious, has made me magnanimous. As far as I am concerned, my moralized lecture has evaporated like so much hot air.

Something has soured here, but what? And how? It is difficult to pinpoint exactly when and where and why my struggle with you over apologizing went awry. At a general level, we were grappling over who is in charge and what each of us can demand—deep struggles, which aren't always unhealthy. There is some level of parent-child struggle over identity that seems more natural than destructive.

I detect a natural, healthier version of such parent-child struggle in Mary's interactions with Jesus during his first miracle. Shortly after Jesus has called his disciples in the Gospel of John, he attends a wedding feast at Cana, along with his mother and the disciples. Late in the feast, his mother comes up to him and informs him there is no wine. Is she passive-aggressively asking for a miracle? Hinting for one? Jesus seems to think so. He responds in what seems to me like irritation: "Woman, what concern is that to you and me? My hour has not yet come."

Mary is not deflated. She offers no response to Jesus's protest, but instead instructs the servants to do whatever Jesus tells them and exits the scene. I love this picture of Mary—cool, authoritative, pragmatic. She has traveled far from the day of her wonder-filled yes to Gabriel, from her amazed pondering of her son's infancy. No longer the ingénue, Mary is full of divine knowing not yet shared by the rest of the world, so she offers her advice: do whatever he tells you to do.

Her words to Jesus and the servants are born out of reverence for her son, whom she has known more intimately than anyone. But still, as a parent-child exchange, the encounter between Mary and Jesus is tense. They do not agree about how he should guard or reveal his identity, about whether his hour has come—or whether helping his neighbors save face is the moment to inaugurate his ministry to the least of these. In the end, he defers to her. He turns water into wine, which becomes, as the Gospel of John says, "the first of his signs . . . [that] revealed his glory." Thus Mary provokes his first miracle, which ends in hints of drunkenness. "Everyone serves the good wine first, and then the inferior wine after the guests have become drunk," the steward says. "But you have kept the good wine until now." Afterwards, Mary travels with Jesus and his disciples to Capernaum.

Jesus's next actions recorded in John's Gospel are not so submissive. He cleanses the Temple with a whip of cords, driving out the money changers and sacrificial animals, overturning tables and spilling coins. The only parent he mentions in this episode is his heavenly Father. With his whip and his zeal, Jesus cleans his Father's house. There is something about the revelation his mother provoked, and the respectful but irritated struggle with her, that led to Jesus publicly claiming his identity as the Son of the Father. The struggle with his mother has, the Gospel of John seems to suggest, led him to his mission in a new way.

In both the wedding feast and Temple-cleansing, Jesus is much older than you are now. You will not have *this kind* of identity contest with me for some time. But our conflicts now are in some ways early versions of those later struggles, struggles over who you will be and how the terms for that identity will be set, struggles over who bears responsibility and risk. Both our current struggles and the later ones can be encounters that wound and bless, like Jacob's striving with the angel at Peniel. During his night with the angel, Jacob receives a blessing; he wounds his thigh; he takes a new name. At daybreak, he is Israel.

There is something about such striving, perhaps even about the wounding and the blessing, that is part and parcel of growing up and taking one's place in the world. Everyone has to jostle about to learn how to accommodate the new identity the child labors to claim. I as your mother decrease so that you may increase. Discerning when and how that happens is uncomfortable.

What I regret is not my annoyance; it is that part of me that does not want to cede ground. My *libido dominandi* does not want you to grow up on terms other than my own, and so that same *libido dominandi* leads me into the fire and ice of rage. But I can imagine a relationship where the struggle is less fraught, where the striving gives way to new forms of relationship, where, like Mary's exchange with Jesus, it helps generate new roles for you in the world. Today I will speak with a therapist.

In the meantime, I reflect on the ways that my lust to dominate is nourished by my shame—a shame that comes to me through the way your life exposes me to the world. By your advent, you birthed new parts of me and dredged up old parts I had suppressed or denied. I was laid bare through your arrival in ways I never had been and would never have chosen.

In the beginning, that exposure was surprisingly physical. Through you, my body became public. The transition began when you were in my womb, and others would feel the growing bump that signaled your presence. Women often comment on this startling feature of pregnancy, that the pregnant body acquires a public significance, and so it seems to invite intimacy other bodies do not. Pregnant women may find their abdomen being touched by acquaintances, colleagues, strangers, people who have never even shaken their hand.

It was strange for me as an adult to be touched like this—though such touching is less strange for you. Babies, toddlers, and small children are quite commonly touched by people. But the touching expectations around children differ. The child in our society is not only touched more than the adult; she can also touch in ways not normal for adults: tickling, hand-holding, lap-sitting, leaning, hanging. The pregnant woman, by contrast, is not welcomed into a life of new, mutual intimacy. Her pregnancy does not authorize her to touch others; only to be touched by them.

In our world, her belly signals that she is uniquely available for public handling. As pregnant, I was exposed.

This new exposure continued as you were born and began to breastfeed. I would take you to parks, churches, and restaurants where I would try to nurse you under a tented nursing cover. When you were very young, I would dip under the tent with you, struggling to help you latch onto my breast as the cover slid on each side, offering little peeks into the drama underneath. As you grew, you often did not like those covers, and so you would grab at the tent and pull it back to expose me to the world. I began to ask myself who this nursing cover protects, anyway? Certainly not you, who hated it. It didn't make my life any easier, either. Was I protecting the public from the horror of seeing a woman's nursing breast? Sometimes I gave up on the tent and tried to nurse you discretely without one. And that would lead to other slips, as you popped off my breast mid-suckle or tried to arrange a better situation for yourself. There was little way around it: to be a nursing mother out in the world was to risk these forms of exposure.

The exposures of belly and breast gave way, when you became an active toddler, to exposures of thigh and buttocks as you developed a habit of tugging on my looser skirts. Sometimes you pulled because you wanted my attention; sometimes you just seemed to be in a mood to hang on me. But there was more than one occasion when I found myself, mid-conversation, hastily readjusting my clothes. Such bodily exposures would unsettle me from my role at the moment—as a teacher, grocery shopper, friend. I clothe myself for these roles, and you undid my costuming, putting me before the world, for a brief moment, without a role to take refuge in. I have a strongly modest sensibility, so accepting these physical exposures was no small change. But my growing practicality and focus on providing care for you combined to energize a new sensibility about my body in the world. I suffered surprisingly little embarrassment over events that would have mortified me before your birth.

For in the end, it was not these physical exposures that proved most difficult for me. They did not elicit a desire to dominate. It was the exposure that came as you grew older, the less literal forms of exposure in which hidden parts of myself are revealed: my need to seem like I have it all together, my desire to please others, my attachment to things going a certain way, my disquiet when these things are threatened. All of this went into generating the scene in the bathroom stall. They provoked my *libido dominandi* as a way of covering myself, finding a fig leaf for this psychic exposure. Addressing your anxieties, and my difficulty with particular anxieties of yours, has revealed to me my own suppressed anxieties. When I am harsh with you, I realize it is often because I see some aspect of what I don't like about myself in you. In my raw desire and its thwarting, you have exposed me to myself and to the world. I am naked and ashamed. My self-image, projected to myself and the world, begins to collapse. I try to make you do what I want so that I can be covered again, to clothe myself in the role and image I prefer.

Since becoming a parent, I think more than I used to about Jesus's nakedness on the cross. It is not something I thought about as a child, when I heard most about the physical pain of crucifixion, as if Jesus's accomplishment on the cross were that of a heroic athlete, suffering tests of his mighty physical endurance. As I grew older and began to read more theological works, I learned to focus on the spiritual abandonment of Christ, by his friends, by his world, by his Father. But lately I am struck by the cross's shame. I am struck by the humiliation of being naked in front of his friends, his enemies, those he taught, those he healed, those who disbelieved his teachings and healings.

The shame of the cross is not just this physical exposure. It is the humiliation of being paraded around as impotent, a parody of himself. His coverings may be more shameful than the nakedness. He is clothed in a scarlet robe and crowned in thorns as the people taunt, "Hail, King of the Jews!" They hurl at him words meant to expose his powerlessness, to reveal him as a fraud. "If you're the Son of God, then come down off the cross." And: "Save yourself, and we will believe you." The Creator of all the universe watches a little piece of creation mock its Creator as a charlatan.

I have described the cross as a shame, but I wonder—was Jesus ashamed in his nakedness? Or by the accusations of weakness and fraud? If shame requires duplicity of who one is and who one wants or seems to be, then the cross cannot be a source of shame for God. What, after all, was there to expose about Christ? Christ hid no secret sin, nor falseness; he did not want to hide himself. If the cross was an exposure of Christ, it was one that simply intensified the revelation of the invisible God begun with the baby in a manger. When humanity tried to bare Christ to the world, Christ did not try to cover himself. Because he is not ashamed, he can respond to exposure, not with domination, but with love. On the cross, Christ reveals the depths of divine love, which travels all the way through violence, cruelty, mockery. At peace with who he is, Christ suffers exposures with love. The shame of the cross is not Christ's; it is ours.

You in your separateness expose my impotence, my fear, my vulnerability. I am weak, and in moments like the locked café bathroom, I despise my weakness. I try to mask it by being stronger than you, compelling you to do what I wish. When you, through your own anxieties, questions, and desires, expose those parts of me I would rather deny, my fury comes quick and strong, and I rush to cover my shame. I am exposed as occasionally ill-at-ease in the world, uncomfortable with myself, and sinful. The exposures both enrage and deflate me, because I have not found peace with myself. They point to the depth of the shame that funds my lust for domination.

My lust for domination is also, queerly, enflamed by my love for you. If I ask what my deepest desire for you is, it is that you have the freedom to love—without reservation, resentment, or anxiety. When I feel my own impotence in helping you toward that vision, I resort to methods that deny who you are and ignore the ways you are separate from me. I try to substitute my will for yours as my lack of peace with myself and my love for you collude in my domination of you. I so deeply want you to flourish that I am tempted to coerce you into freedom. I see the irony. I know that it is a fool's errand to dominate you in order to make you free and that my temptation to do so will only take me to that familiar swamp of love and shame and anger. But my anxiety about your flourishing and freedom incites the spirit of domination I find so difficult to resist.

I want to be like Mary, whose provocations and struggles with her child were uncomfortable, perhaps irritating, but ultimately led Jesus to claim his identity in a new and powerful way. I want to struggle with you in a way that blesses you, that leads you into better versions of yourself. I wonder what Monica felt, watching Augustine moving away from the Catholic Church in his time with the Manichees. Augustine writes that she "wept over [him] as a person dead"—not only dead, but also one who might possibly live again, one "to be revived by you." In Monica's constant waiting, in her sadness and anxiety about her son's well-being, was she ever tempted to exercise manipulative forms of control over her son's life? (Did she?) When Augustine finally breaks free from the Manichees by finding the Platonists, Monica is not overly impressed. As Augustine writes, "[S]he did not leap for joy." She was waiting for another conversion, one for which she "daily and tearfully prayed."

Though Monica was not thrilled about Augustine's dalliance with the Platonists, Platonism was an important type of therapy for Augustine. It helped him exorcise his false idea of God as physical entity stretched thinly out across the universe. With the Platonists, he began to grasp what it means to claim God is spirit and to untangle the problem of evil. They help him develop a truer picture of God. They do not, Augustine also points out, teach him all of God's story. Specifically, they do not teach that in Christ, God became flesh.

The chapter on the Platonists has a prominent place in the *Confessions*, just before the chapter culminating in his conversion in the Garden of Milan. Every time I teach it, I ask my students why these stories of lust and the Platonists are threaded together. What does learning that God is spirit, but that God also became flesh, have to do with Augustine's ceasing from lust and healing his will? Unlike many of my questions, I ask this one innocently. The intertwining seems so right to me and still I feel that I haven't gotten to the bottom of it. Is it just an intellectual journey that runs on a separate track from the journey of the will? Or do these intellectual transformations energize or pressure the conversion of the will? What does Augustine learn from the Platonists about living his life in the flesh?

It is time for my own therapy. The therapist is young and childless. We talk about the bathroom stall and other parenting failures; she recommends books to me. Her background is in neurobiology, and she gives me a brief tutorial on the brain and how it works. We have different levels to our brains, she says: the reptilian brain, the mammalian brain, and the human brain. When we are afraid, our reptilian brain takes over and channels us to one of its three instincts, fight, flight, or shut down. When we are hungry or tired, we operate out of our mammalian brain. Only when we feel safe and our needs are met can we process higher level information in our human brain. Looking at her brain illustrations, I wonder what neurobiologists might help me see about fleshly life.

The picture is supposed to help me grasp that punishing or instructing you while you are operating out of your reptilian brain or even your mammalian brain is ineffective. You cannot choose the good when you are caught in anxiety. Constrained by the signals of your reptilian brain, your will is frozen, or madly dispersed; it cannot move toward the good until it thaws and gathers. I see the way this picture of you, of us together, is one that registers not just the separateness of your emotional life and needs, but their bodily existence as well. To shepherd your soul, I, too, must take seriously your bodily life and condition. My attempts to dominate you are ways of denying your bodiliness, efforts to force your will to override its own biological existence.

Over the next several weeks, I begin to hear the therapist's picture of the brain described everywhere: in lectures by traveling parent experts, in articles I encounter, in other parents I talk to. It seems new, but it has many precedents. I see, for example, the way it harmonizes with the vision of education practiced by Maria Montessori. What Montessori wants for children is what I think I want: perfect freedom, the freedom to reject rewards of unjust systems and to suffer punishment for worthy causes, the freedom to be determined by something altogether greater and more internal than reward and punishment. She wants, in sum, children to have the freedom of a saint—the freedom of perfect love, love without fear or grasping, love determined not by coercion but by its own orientation to the good. Montessori is famous for her philosophy of the prepared environment, in which children flourish when the environment is suited to their own bodies and minds, and yet the preparation she finds most important concerns neither furniture nor tools nor space. It is the preparation of the caregiver. If what I want for you is freedom, then I must root out pride, anger, and impatience from my heart. By these vices, I turn away from you and your needs.

How can I prepare myself to care for you? How can I stop turning away from you, to be present to you in your neediness and possibility? I want to imitate Christ, who suffers exposure without turning from the way of perfect love. I want to resist the temptation to grasp and coerce, to wait patiently and hopefully for new life to work its way into your heart and mine. I want to suffer your freedom, as Christ suffers mine. This freedom, I know, risks failure. You may never apologize.

I look back to Montessori for guidance. How do Montessori classrooms handle apologies? In teaching children to say they're sorry, they do not resort to rewards and punishment. They have a peace rug, where the aggrieved children come together and tell their stories to one another about why they feel wronged. They are brought face to face with the hurt they have caused and given an opportunity to acknowledge that pain, apologize for it, and ask what they can do to make it right. The hope is not to teach children to say the words "I'm sorry," which many people learn to do hypocritically or manipulatively and which, especially, many girls grow up to do habitually in a gesture of self-effacement. The hope is to lead children to a disposition of proper sorrow for injury.

I like this approach, but your problem is not that you fail to feel sorrow. I often see the regret in your face. You feel sorrow, but you will not, or cannot, communicate it. You are frozen by fear, which you sometimes express like anger. It frustrates, troubles, and saddens me to see you deflect your shame, as if you cannot bear to draw near enough to your own emotion to articulate it.

What I learn from neurobiology about how children flourish rhymes with what I learn from other sources of knowledge, those given not by nature but by grace. From Christ, I see you cannot learn freedom from domination. And I see the way you are more than the occasion of my sin or the object of my lust to dominate. But life with you can also train me in a different way—a way of loving without grasping and living exposed without frantically covering. It is not just that I am learning to adjust myself so that you can be free, but these adjustments teach me how to be free as well. Life with you dramatizes to me my own unfreedom. And I want to be free—free to love, free to show myself, free to offer my torments as laboring pains in a mental pregnancy.

I also want you to learn to apologize. I know that you both do and do not want to. I know that your will is not mine. What can I do? My will cannot triumph here; that would not help you into saintly freedom. But your will is entangled in some fear I do not understand. Not my will but thine must choose the good. I try a different tack.

On a happy afternoon, we sit down and talk about why you cannot say you are sorry. You don't know. You just can't. I think about that claim and try to accept it. You can write it, you say, hopefully. I nod. That is a step. But there are times when you need to apologize right on the spot, I point out. What can we do then? We are both silent for a while. Can you say, "I apologize?" You pause and then nod tentatively. You think so. We brainstorm other possibilities together. You can say, "I regret," or, "I wish I hadn't." You cannot say, "Please forgive me." Then I apologize for becoming so angry about your refusal to apologize. I ask if you can apologize for not apologizing. You look at me with a pained expression and say in a small voice, "I apologize."

It's a temporary compromise. I am sure it will not be the last of our negotiations, on this subject or many more. I know, too, it will not be the last time I struggle over what it means that we have two separate wills, my adult will and your will-in-development, which has to be both respected and instructed. I am not sure how

I'll cultivate your will over the years, but I do know that I have to give up some illusory vision of my sovereignty over you.

I am, in many ways, still learning to become two. Several years ago now, my body became two as you were born and took on a separate bodily life from mine. And since that physical labor I have been in periodic episodes of spiritual labor for you, learning to help birth your selfhood, your spiritual self, your sovereignty, as distinct from my own.

Facing your freedom, I come to terms with the nature of my own, the way it exists embedded in and with the freedoms of others, the way that freedom is paradoxically made possible by the ways I depend upon others and risk my exposure to them. In this way, daughter, your freedom teaches me something about who I am in relation to God, and how I can move more deeply into that identity. By your freedom, I learn to be God's child, and through that childhood, I learn how to be a more faithful parent. I want to be unwavering in my loving presence to you, to resist the seductions of domination and the temptations to cover myself, so as to give myself to both you and God, to say to you both, "Here I am."

CHAPTER 8

Conversion

But my madness with myself was part of the process of
recovering health, and in the agony of death I was
coming to life.

"Here I am" is the faithful one's response to the call of the Lord. Abraham, Jacob, Joseph, Moses, Samuel, Isaiah, Mary—all answer the Lord or the Lord's emissaries with this affirmation of presence. "Here I am" welcomes God and expresses receptiveness to a mission yet unknown. It is a yes given before any charge is made or question asked. Throughout the Old Testament, this call and response recurs in a simple liturgy that reaffirms the human-divine relation. God calls the holy person's name, and she responds *Hineni*. "Here I am." But there are revealing variations on this call and response.

One variation comes in Genesis, the first time the call and response appears in Scripture. Here there is only call, no response. Adam and Eve are in the Garden of Eden after they have eaten the forbidden fruit. They are hiding from God, and so God calls to Adam, "Where are you?" The question invites the response, "Here I am." But instead, Adam answers that he heard the Lord coming and hid himself in shame. Then Adam and Eve cover their exposure with excuses for their sin and are ultimately expelled from the intimate presence of the God they attempted to skirt. God clothes them, taking away the sting of their shame, and they leave the garden to toil and to till. The "here I am" that Adam does not offer haunts the rest of God's story with the people of God, as a new estrangement grows up between the once easy intimacy of God and humanity. Prophets and other holy people work to repair the rupture in this relation, laboring to overcome the absence that clouds a once clear and mutual presence. The failed "here I am" marks life under the rule of sin.

The second variation occurs one of the last times "here I am" appears in the Old Testament. It is in the book of Isaiah, and the difference this time is that "here I am" does not come from the mouth of a human saying it to God—though that happened earlier in the book, during Isaiah's call to prophecy. It is God who says "here I am" to God's people. In the vision of true worship Isaiah describes, the people feed the hungry, shelter the poor, and do not hide from their neighbors. Then they glow with glory and find healing. Isaiah goes on to describe to the people what this glory and healing look like. "Then you shall call, and the Lord will answer; you shall cry for help, and he will say, Here I am." It is as if God supplies the attentive presence Adam and Eve could not muster—or as if the people of God learn how to receive divine presence through practicing greater attention and care for one another. Perhaps in caring for the vulnerable, they learn to hear the voice of the Lord who always says, "Here I am." They may even learn to say those words to God then as well.

This affirmation of presence requires a stillness that contrasts with the frantic madness of my tornado within. Even now my thoughts swirl around the image of us locked in that café bathroom. I want to put the incident behind me, but I keep returning to a mental picture of me willing you to apologize, ignoring your tears, hardening myself against your pain. The picture seems to stand for something in my relationship to you that has not gone away, despite my attempt to turn from my baser impulses, and so my thoughts keep whipping around it, gathering other memories and mental images into their whirlwind. I see in the swirling chaos other moments in our relationship when I manipulated you with guilt or goaded you with rewards. I remember freezing a batch of chocolate chip cookies as big as your hand to use as incentive for you to apologize. When the occasion called for your apology, I brought out the cookies and promised you one if you would just say the words. Was the reward a potentially helpful way to correct a bad habit? A distortion of the act of apology? The answer turned out to be immaterial. You never apologized; the cookies just made you more upset. After six weeks and at least two meltdowns, I ate the cookies one night after you went to bed.

I see the way that the cookies, wise or not, were connected with my lust to dominate. At times I want to move you like a limb of the soul. In my attempts to save you from suffering and vice, I end up corrupting that impulse, inflicting suffering on you and modeling vicious habits. I am exhausted by my habits of domination, and still I find myself falling into them again and again. How can I quit damaging you? How can I accept, finally and for all time, your separateness and your freedom? We are entering Holy Week, and I feel anything but holy.

My phone buzzes with an alert. It's a pastoral care email from our Protestant church. My thoughts turn to Pastor Nora, who has been fostering a baby girl she hopes to adopt. I have been meaning to sort through your old clothes and baby toys to put together a box for her. My thoughts are halfway to the boxes where I've stored your baby things when I pick up my phone to open the email. It is from the associate pastor. A relative has unexpectedly come forward to claim Samantha and will likely be granted permanent custody of her. Pastor Nora will not be back for Holy Week, as she will instead prepare to say good-bye to Samantha. She is grieving and would like our prayers. The email ends abruptly. I read it a second and then a third time, breathless.

"Mommy?" You call, but I am lost in my thoughts, staring at my phone. "Mommy, are you okay?" You call for me several times before I finally turn and see you looking worriedly at my face. I take you in my arms. You are not so small as you once were, nor so round. The chubbiness of early childhood has given way to a body that seems to be all limbs. We sit in our old rocking chair, swinging like we did in your babyhood. I stroke your back and tell you I'm fine, everything is fine. I will tell you about Samantha later.

Rocking you, I find myself wanting to rationalize the situation, as if in finding a logic to it, I can keep its painfulness from leaching into my life. I tell myself Pastor Nora knew it was possible the adoption would not go through. She knew Samantha was not yet her baby. But what does it mean for any baby to be "ours?" In what sense are you *mine*? You are not my property; you are not my own body. You are not mine to possess or control—though that is how I am tempted to relate to you. My legal rights are different from those of a foster parent, but how different, really, is my claim on you?

I recoil at this thought that you are not fully mine. Pastor Nora's preparation to surrender Samantha to a relative is pressing some anxiety in me, pulling back the curtain on my own graspingness. I glimpse the ugliness of my soul. Selfishness infects my love for you. The love of a foster parent who can cherish her charge and yet lovingly send her on is an image, really, of all parental love—of how my love for you should be. You are, in an important sense, not my own; you are separate from me. But I feel paralyzed by my own refusal to let you be separate from me. To admit your separateness is to know I can lose you.

Later that week we arrive at a crowded church—our Catholic church—for Maundy Thursday. As we thread our way through the busy foyer, I catch fragments of conversation. One woman, standing with her arm around another, is saying that she was consoled by the Blessed Virgin on the anniversary loss of her son. "She has been such a comfort to me," the woman says, grasping with her free hand the fingers of her friend. I find both strange and beautiful the way some Catholics have of speaking about long-dead religious figures as if they are friends next door. I am never quite sure how to interpret it. Is it a metaphorical way of speaking, a way of expressing how the stories of saints bring solace? Do they experience themselves as literally seeing and feeling these figures? Do they enter a kind of vision or trance, in which saints appear to them? Or is it some movement of heart and mind, which they can name as the presence of Mary or Christ or a saint? I wonder about the way Mary is present to this woman and whether her presence is similar to how Antony was present to Augustine and Ponticianus in their conversions.

Someday I mean to ask about this, but not today. We hurry in to find you a seat near the front, where you can see the altar. As Mass begins, you look attentively around, busy with standing up, sitting down, crossing yourself, and singing. When we stand for the gospel reading, you lean against me and pull out your own Bible, which is styled like a graphic novel, and, ignoring the priest, turn to the second chapter of Luke. I look over your shoulder to see the story of Mary, Joseph, and Jesus in pilgrimage to the Temple in Jerusalem. Familiar as the story is, the narrative arrests me as if it is new. As we sit down for the homily, I find Luke 2 in your father's missal and read it for myself.

Jesus is twelve, considerably older than you are now, during his family's annual Passover journey to the Temple. They must have been traveling in a great crowd because when they begin their return trip, Jesus's parents do not realize Jesus is absent. Luke calmly reports the situation. "Assuming that he was in the group of travelers, they went a day's journey. Then they started to look for him among their relatives and friends. When they did not find him, they returned to Jerusalem to search for him."

Luke's words march along as slowly and steadily as a caravan, continuing the even pace at which he narrates all the events surrounding this one. But I can imagine Mary's anxious thoughts flying through possibilities. *Where did I last see him? Wasn't he at breakfast this morning? Did he go off with that child he was playing with in Jerusalem?* I picture her trying not to think the thought that keeps knocking on her mind: *Has the hour of his persecution arrived?* Mary and Joseph find their boy three days later—a terrible three days of loss that foreshadows another still more terrible three days of loss to come years later. Jesus is sitting with the rabbis, listening, questioning, and amazing all with his understanding. His parents, Luke writes, are astonished. Relief explodes from Mary like anger, "Child, why have you treated us like this? Look, your father and I have been searching for you in great anxiety."

I can identify with Mary in this story. Her emotions are in her words and actions, her presence here as always narrated alongside the child Jesus. But, for the first time reading this story, I also wonder about how Joseph experiences this moment, what it is like for him to be the father of the Christ. His presence is silent and unmarked. Luke gives us no words of Joseph's, here or elsewhere in the gospel. Neither is there any sentence in all of Luke about what Joseph is doing, though his actions are sometimes included under descriptions of what Jesus's parents are doing (losing Jesus, searching for him). The story of Jesus's childhood in Luke is all about Mary—Mary's *Magnificat*, Mary's visit to her kinswoman, Mary's ponderings, Mary's relief. Joseph is a minor figure.

Joseph's name, in fact, appears in just five places in Luke. In addition to one invocation of his name when Jesus teaches in the synagogue, Joseph is mentioned as Mary's betrothed, as one whose lineage tracks back to David's city of Bethlehem, and as the companion of Mary and Jesus at the manger. By offering Mary the shelter of marriage and by establishing Jesus's birth city, Joseph helps provide an earthly home for these two larger-than-life characters, God and the Mother of God. But he is not a major character in the gospels; he has no grand scenes. Joseph plays a slightly larger role in the Gospel of Matthew, which mentions that when he found out Mary was pregnant, he planned to divorce her quietly, to spare her the pain of public humiliation. An angel appears to him in a dream and tells him to take Mary as his wife. He wakes and obeys, wordlessly.

Newly attuned to Joseph's experience, I am caught short by Jesus's response to Marys' rebuke. He is unabashed and unregretful. (I try not to imagine myself getting into an apology war with boy Jesus.) He is not even defensive. Perhaps he is genuinely puzzled as he asks, "Why were you searching for me? Did you not know that I must be in my Father's house?"

"My Father's house." Did that reply sting Joseph, who had assumed the role of father in Jesus's life, even without many of the proud moments of fatherhood? Instead of celebrating his fiancée's pregnancy, he quietly endures the shame of appearing cuckolded. Instead of using his carpentry skills to make his child's first crib, he scavenges a barn to make do with a food trough. He provides for a holy family from which he is, in some sense, estranged; he has not the flesh-and-blood connection to the God-child his wife does. He has a divine child and a wife who gave that divine child her very flesh. His own proximity to divinity is not so intimate as his wife's; his claim to the family is more open to question.

Mary's yes is often celebrated as a moment of supreme human obedience, but what of Joseph's silent assent? Her sacrifice is dramatically represented in pietàs, but what of Joseph's humbler, quotidian sacrifices? I think Joseph must have been a man who knew how to open up his desires toward God's call into the unknown. In submitting to the superiority of Mary's calling, by taking her as his wife, Joseph is revered as a saint. But surpassing him, Mary becomes the Queen of Heaven, the Mother of God, the Star of the Sea. He must have been a gentle man, and kind. Perhaps for his great humility, God spared him his son's crucifixion.

In light of Joseph's role, Jesus's reply to Mary at this moment seems to me almost cruel. In the phrase "my Father's house," the boy Jesus sidelines his earthly adoptive father, minimizing both his claims to fatherhood and the house this carpenter has provided for his son. When Luke mentions Joseph after that episode, it is in Jesus's genealogy, and even as he records Joseph's ancestry, Luke also minimizes Joseph's claim on Jesus, writing, Jesus "was the son (as was thought) of Joseph." The final time Joseph is mentioned by name in the gospel occurs after Jesus teaches in the synagogue, proclaiming for those congregated that Isaiah's prophecy has been fulfilled before them. The gathered respond in amazement, "Is not this Joseph's son?" "Joseph" here signifies a certain lowliness that contrasts with Jesus's impressive display. The question might, too, speak to father and son's difference in manner. Where Jesus seems drawn to teaching, interpreting, and prophesying, I cannot imagine Joseph often read and proclaimed Scriptures in front of an audience. I could be wrong, but his presence is so lightly registered in the gospels that it is difficult to imagine him having a commanding presence anywhere.

What can I make of Jesus's stark words to his father? Perhaps like the wine miracle, the encounter at the Temple is part of the striving of the parent-child relationship, the wounding and blessing by which a child takes his place in the world. But if Joseph is wounded, he does not express it in Luke's gospel; he maintains his silence until he disappears altogether after that last mention in the synagogue. His death is not even recorded. How did it happen? Was Jesus there when he died? How did his wife and son mourn him? We do not know. Joseph simply fades from view. While there are traditions, feasts, and places associated with the end of Mary's earthly life, there are none that I know of for Joseph. When Jesus himself dies, he is buried in the tomb of a different, wealthier Joseph, who gives him the fine burial place his father could not. I confess: I could not have raised the God-child with the gentle humility of Joseph, nor have had the grace to overlook my apparent unimportance in my child's life.

I come home from Mass that night, and as your father puts you to sleep, I pick up my Bible and thumb through its pages. In his graciousness and unpossessive parental presence, Joseph may be an aberration in our world—but nestled in the stories of Scripture, the narrative around Joseph sounds a familiar motif. It is a minor theme in Scripture, but a real one, the way children are gifts we cannot possess. All the stories of barren women whose wombs are opened by God—including the story of Israel that begins with God opening the barren womb of the aged Sarah—testify to the way that children come as gifts we never claim as wholly our own. When we do try to possess them, or when parental love goes awry, trouble develops. Jacob loved the first Joseph, the Joseph of Genesis, in such a way that he unwittingly endangers him and must suffer his loss for many years. Hannah, by contrast, knows her son is a gift.

Hannah's barrenness was a source of great grief to her. Worshiping and sacrificing in Shiloh, she vows that if the Lord gives her a son, she will in turn give him to the Lord as a Nazirite. She weeps so bitterly and prays so intensely that the priest Eli rebukes her for drunkenness. When she responds that she has been praying out of her anxiety and sorrow, he takes pity on her. Whether out of that pity, or to induce her to leave, or both, he says, "Go in peace; the God of Israel grant the petition you have made to him." Hannah makes good on her vow. As soon as she weans her son, she brings him back to the house of the Lord at Shiloh and "leaves him there for the Lord." As she departs from her much-wanted son, she expresses no despondency. Instead, she sings a song of exultation to the Lord, not unlike Mary's *Magnificat*. Every year thereafter, she returns to Shiloh to make a sacrifice to the Lord and to bring her son Samuel a new cloak. How can Hannah's leaving Samuel at a temple not remind me of Mary and Joseph losing Jesus at a Temple centuries later?

I want to receive you as a gift. I know how I often fail that desire. I want to be Hannah, she of the free offering, of the joyful reception of her child. But instead I find myself falling back into bad habits, my good resolutions lost to a compulsion to treat you as an extension of my own fierce will.

I flip back to the gospels. The Hannah story is echoed in Mary's life in more ways than one. It is not just that Mary's *Magnificat* echoes Hannah's song but that Hannah's story provides a narrative structure for how the church often tells the story of Mary's parents, whom it names Anna and Joachim. Like Hannah, they are childless for many years, and also like Hannah, they give their loved child to God for life in the Temple. Their gift to the Temple becomes the gift of the church. Mary gives her flesh and blood to the God who comes to dwell among us. As the first earthly home of Christ, Mary's body is the first church.

The story of Jesus's birth in the gospel of Matthew is a more sinister tale, which elaborates a more violent connection between the birth of Christ and the stories of Israel. Matthew's story of the slaughter of the innocents and the Holy Family's flight through Egypt brings me back, once again, to Moses, whose story has become so poignant to me since becoming a mother. Recalling Pharaoh during Moses's infancy, Herod calls for the slaughter of all children in Bethlehem under the age of two. Moses's unnamed mother hid him for three months, but when she can no longer keep him safe by hiding, she seeks a new way to help him live. She plasters a papyrus basket, puts her baby in it, and places the basket in some reeds at the bank of the river where Pharaoh's daughter was bathing. I admire not just the courage and hope but the canniness of this plan. It follows the letter of the law. Pharaoh had commanded that all baby boys be thrown into the Nile, and here this babe is indeed in the Nile. When Pharaoh's daughter sees the boy and hears his plaintive cries, she has pity on him, takes him in her arms, and names him. Moses's sister Miriam had been watching, and when she sees Pharaoh's daughter intends to save the child's life, she offers to find a wet nurse, who is, of course, Moses's actual mother. Moses stays with his mother until he is weaned and then returns to Pharaoh's daughter.

I wonder if Miriam thought about this moment where Pharaoh's daughter draws her baby brother from the water when, years later, that same brother crosses the miraculously parted Red Sea with his people, leading them from slavery into freedom. Did she ponder the miracle of the Lord who saves Moses's life through the water as an infant and again through water saves Moses and the people of God? Was her mother with her at the time? Did she weep with joy, seeing that in giving up her son to a different people, with a different religion, in order to save him, she had received him back as a leader of her own people and her own religion? Perhaps she had died by then, and Miriam thinks of her mother's sacrifice and its vindication with gladness. Scripture says that Miriam takes a tambourine and sings a song, dancing in joy to the Lord. *The horse and the rider God has cast into the sea.* It is another foreshadow of the *Magnificat*, when Mary sings, *God has scattered the proud in the thoughts of their hearts. The Lord has brought down the powerful from their thrones.*

Against the narratives of these loving, courageous parents, I see my own shortcomings all the more clearly. I want to renounce my own grasping desire, to practice instead their loving attention, but it is so difficult. No, that is not precise. It is often easy to attend to you lovingly, but it is difficult to stay in that mode, especially when I am stressed, tired, and discouraged. It is so easy, in those moments, to slip toward domination or neglect. Though domination is aggressive and neglect passive, both are two faces of a similar event: the withdrawal from the reality of your presence. As in my struggles wanting you to apologize, I can deny you and your claims on me by neglecting you—looking away from your needs, shutting out your desires, minimizing your pain—or I can deny you and your claims on me by dominating you, by substituting my own claims for yours. Staying with you in all your needs and desires, abiding with you in such a way that I help to open your particular little self to God, saying to you truthfully at each moment, "Here I am"—that is difficult. The thought of making myself so available and vulnerable to you fatigues me. I go to sleep, both longing and fearing to be like Hannah, Joseph, Mary, and Moses's mother.

On the next day, Good Friday, you ask me to read a story to you from your Bible—not the one like a graphic novel but the one you received when you were younger, that is like a children's book. You turn to the binding of Isaac, the *Akedah*, which is cheerfully illustrated in bright colors and told so as to emphasize the happy ending. But you will not be distracted from the more menacing notes in this tale. You want to know why Isaac's daddy wanted to kill him. I wonder what I am doing, protecting you from the news when I expose you to the world's most appalling realities in Bible stories. There is something about the children's Bible that has made the story more sinister by grinning over the darkness, so I open an adult Bible for us to read. I work through it aloud with you, hoping insight from on high will inspire me as we talk together.

Isaac is the first son of the great family, the first son of Abraham and Sarah. They have been waiting so long for the gift of a son, they sometimes doubted he would ever come. When Isaac arrives in their old age, he is a source of joy and gladness. They name him laughter. I imagine he still seems like a miracle to them well into his boyhood. I imagine Sarah periodically going up to him and embracing him, assuring herself that he is flesh and blood, that he is really, finally here. Isaac looks up at her with affection and exasperation, used to these surprise caresses, as he mildly protests his mother's attentions. I imagine Abraham looking at his son in wonder as he ponders the great nation being established through him. He takes Isaac outside and shows him the night sky, with all of its stars, and repeats to him the promise he received from God. Abraham and Sarah are both filled with love for him, for the gift of God that he is.

But what does it mean to receive a child as a gift? How does a parent resist possessing her child as her own? One day God calls his servant. "Abraham!" And Abraham answers, "Here I am." God tells Abraham to offer Isaac as a sacrifice on a mountain in Moriah. Abraham obeys, traveling up the mountain with his son as Isaac becomes increasingly uneasy. Isaac calls, "Father!" Abraham answers his son as he did the Lord. "Here I am." I heard an interview in which a novelist pointed to this parallelism as a contradiction. "[I]t's a very poignant moment," the novelist said.

"But it's also a paradoxical moment because you cannot be un-conditionally present for a God who wants you to kill your son, while being unconditionally present for your son."

I am not convinced by this reading. I take it the repetition of "here I am" to God and son expresses Abraham's faith that being present to both will not prove impossible, that, somehow, fidelity to God and to Isaac are not in competition with one another, despite appearances. The parallelism emerges from Abraham's faith that God's call to him and Isaac's call to him are not different calls, that he can hear the call of God in Isaac, and will discover how the two calls to faithfulness converge. Perhaps it is even his faith that God has come to him in Isaac, in a way reminiscent of how God came to him in the three mysterious strangers he hosted. When Isaac asks his nervous question about where the sacrifice is, Abraham articulates some version of this faith that his presence to Isaac and God are both possible: "God himself will provide the lamb for a burnt offering, my son." And God, at the last minute, does. The knife is raised when God calls him, "Abraham, Abraham!" For the third time, Abraham answers, "Here I am."

Abraham does not sacrifice Isaac, and God does provide the burnt offering. I interpret this last-minute provision of the ram, not as God changing God's mind, nor as Abraham winning some kind of prize for passing a faith test (though the text does occa-sionally suggest something like this). I take it that God is acting like a teacher here, dramatizing for Abraham what it means to receive a person as gift, and to give oneself as gift. It is not an of-fering unto death but life because God is the Lord of life. Other gods may want us to show devotion by destroying ourselves or the ones we love. But the God of Abraham does not traffic in death-dealing devotion.

To receive you as a gift from God and to receive you as your own, separate self—these are two sides of the same event. This was Abraham's faith, that Isaac was a gift and a separate person, so that even when he was asked to curtail Isaac's freedom by literally binding him, he knew that somehow, this binding could not be for the death of his son—that it must, even more mysteriously, be for his son's freedom. Isaac's life and freedom are not *for* Abraham. He is a gift to Abraham, not a possession for him. Isaac's life is *for* Isaac (and for Isaac by also being for God). Abraham's faith that it is not a contradiction to say "Here I am" to both God and his child—to give his presence fully to both—is his faith that his child is not a fantasy, nor a means to prove his faith. He is a person made by the hands of God, loved by God, given by God, and so he is a character in his own story and God's. He is not a prop in Abraham's life. Abraham's claim to Isaac that God will provide the sacrifice is his faith that Isaac is fully real.

Perhaps it was that faith that got him through the binding of his son. (What did Isaac do? I wonder silently. Did he resist the ropes around him? Was his father assuring him all the time that the Lord would make a way? Was there a physical struggle between them, or did Isaac show absolute trust in the father tying him with ropes?) It is when the knife is raised above bound Isaac, just when things seem bleakest, just when it seems God has abandoned God's plan for a great nation, that God intervenes, making a new way and blessing Abraham. This is the kind of God I am, the Lord seems to say. I make new ways in the darkest hour; I ask for gifts unto life, not offerings of death. The *Akedah* tells me something about what it means to offer you; it means I do not abandon you to death, but offer you up to greater life, greater blessing.

That, at least, is the sense I can make of the story just now. It is the sense I try to impart to you. I tell you that the stories of parents giving their children to God are not just stories of parent-child partings; they are stories of parents receiving back their children in new and unexpected ways. They are, in this way, different from the gut-wrenching stories of immigrant children separated from their parents we have been following on the news. All the children offered up—Isaac, Moses, Samuel, Mary, Christ—become blessings to their parents and their people. You look at me confused, so I repeat the punch line: God wanted to teach Abraham about who God is, that God does *not* demand that children be killed; Abraham loves God well by answering both God's call and the call of his child. You nod okay, though you don't seem wholly assured. We say prayers, and I kiss your forehead as I leave the room.

How do I love you well, as a gift? How do I become free of my *libido dominandi*? In his battle with lust, Augustine strives to lay hold of the deep freedom by which he can will one thing wholly. Through book after book of the *Confessions*, he struggles to bring his divided will from dissipation into unity. Toward the end, he becomes free in a way that allows him to give himself to God in love. He gives to and receives from God his self. There is a paradox running throughout the *Confessions*, as an illusory freedom gives way to a substantial one. In grasping at his self and in orienting his life around his self, Augustine loses it; in releasing that grasp and centering his life around God, Augustine finds his self. It is, in one way, a long riff on Jesus's saying in Matthew and Luke that the one who seeks to save her life will lose it, but the one who loses her life for my sake will save it.

Though I am riven by internal struggle, my drama in helping bring your will into maturity is not quite the same as Augustine's drama with his own will. Battling his corrupt impulses, Augustine grows anxious about the way his loves deviate from God, about how, therefore, his will is set against itself. His divided will means that he lacks wholeness and integrity. He is dissipated, multiple, not identical with himself. I am also multiple; motherhood is its own dissipation, its own "going to pieces" as Maggie Nelson puts it. Your will is not identical to mine, and it will never, post-pregnancy, be identical to mine. Our healing will not come in a divine grace that reunites us, bringing you back into my womb for us to live by one wholly integrated will. My grace is to wait, to love you through the detours your life takes, even if you travel far from me; to be present to you in hope and prayer; and to bring you near Love by reflecting love to you. I can help birth your will into freedom and goodness chiefly by being reborn into such freedom and goodness myself.

Even as my struggle diverges from Augustine's, there is also resonance between his drama and the dramas of parenthood. Parenthood is also a meditation on the strange claim that to save your life you must lose it, and in losing it, you find it. It is a study in renunciations and gifts. When I became a parent, I renounced my own desires as the center of my life; yours—your desires to eat, to cuddle, to sleep—became more fundamental than my own. But as you grow up, I am slowly renouncing your desires as the center of my life, as I teach you how to discern and fulfill them yourself. Having fought so hard for the first renunciation, it is often difficult to manage the second.

You are mine; you are not mine. I think again of Pastor Nora, her pain and her love, and the way all parenting is like foster parenting. But I cannot fully fathom what it must be like to live under the threat of parting with my child. No one will emerge to take you away from me unless I stray woefully from my parenting duties. No, I am not like a foster parent. It is, instead, like Pastor Nora's fostering is an icon for me of what my parenting you could and should be, the way that I should hold you without clutching you as my own, embrace you without claiming you as my possession. I check in on her via Facebook and find that today, on this Good Friday, she has presented baby Samantha to the child's relatives. Pastor Nora has posted a good-bye message filled with love and sorrow for the child she had wanted for her own. She includes photos of herself kissing Samantha's hands, fingers, and toes as the babe leaves her home.

Parenthood demands a kind of asceticism, but, like all asceticism, its end is extravagance. The asceticism of fasting prepares a person to enter more deeply into the joy of the great heavenly banquet. The asceticism of living simply teaches dependence upon others and declutters one's heart, and so helps a person enter into greater friendship with God and fellow creatures. These forms of asceticism, like parenthood, ultimately want, not the renunciation of certain goods, but the laying claim to still greater ones—happiness, community, life abundant, and, especially, the presence of God. That you are not mine to possess, that you are not mine to craft and shape, that you are a gift to me, means that you can also be a divine presence to me. When you call to me in your need, that is God's call to me as well. The space I give you to grow and flourish becomes also the space for my own growth and flourishing. I want to be free of my *libido dominandi*, free to allow us to become these flourishing selves. How can I lay hold of such freedom? Reflecting on his conversion, Augustine writes, "But where through so many years was my freedom of the will? From what deep and hidden recess was it called out in a moment?" In my own life, I have already received and betrayed many moments of calling and recalling me to freedom. My freedom slinks away from me.

I am cleaning now, which I often do when I feel overwhelmed. Cleaning helps me to stay calm, to bring order to our home when I feel internally disordered. When I clean, I can turn my attention elsewhere, beyond my sadness. I hang up jackets, put away toys, sweep the floor. Order emerges. The world is a little bit better. Sometimes I even rediscover lost treasures: coins, small toys, once-cherished crafts. This evening, I look under the couch and find a little painted wooden Macrina figure, a peg doll of your special saint, whom I return to so often in my thoughts of you.

You hold her during prayer sometimes, and I like to watch you with her. Though I have never told you this, I have since you were born thought of Macrina as your secret name, the way Macrina's mother Emmelia gave her the secret name of Thecla.

When Emmelia was pregnant with Macrina, after she had been in labor with her and just before she delivered her, she fell asleep. She dreamt she held the child in her womb in her hands, and an angel—someone "in form and raiment more splendid than a human being"—called the child Thecla. Thecla was a famous saint who was sentenced to death by wild beasts for attacking a nobleman assaulting her. She not only survived the beasts, but she baptized herself in the arena and then took off for adventures with the Apostle Paul. The vision of the angel calling her baby Thecla appeared to Emmelia three times. Emmelia wakes, and the labor to birth her daughter goes easily; soon her dream is realized as the babe is placed in her arms. She names her daughter Macrina and keeps Thecla as her secret name.

Over the course of her life, Emmelia realizes what it means that Macrina's secret name is Thecla. They are close, this mother-daughter pair. Macrina, after all, is the one Emmelia jokes about carrying with her always and everywhere. When Macrina comes of age, Emmelia agrees to marry her off, but Macrina demurs when her fiancé dies. She stays in the home, near her mother. But the cost of that closeness is that Macrina makes Emmelia's entire life strange, freeing their servants and turning their home into a convent. To allow Macrina's will to flourish is to agree to have her own life upended. Their ongoing mother-daughter drama is performed in the episode around Macrina's cancerous breast, and in Macrina's death, when she glows beneath her mother's mantel. In life and death, they circle around one another, learning to acknowledge each other's separateness, losing and gaining one another in different ways, refusing to hold each other as possessions.

Augustine and Monica have a still more complicated relationship, but one that attains an interesting mutuality just before she dies, when a conversation between them leads to contemplation in which they attain "the region of inexhaustible abundance." Augustine writes, "There life is the wisdom by which all creatures come into being, both things which were and which will be." Shortly after this vision of life and the eternal wisdom that lies beyond it, Monica dies. Monica and Augustine attain their greatest unity with one another as Augustine also attains his greatest unity with God in the narrative of the *Confessions*. His drama seems so different than mine: he is moving from separation from God and mother to unity with both; I am learning to move into separateness with you so that we can both move into unity with God. I cannot have the Macrina-Emmelia unity nor the Augustine-Monica unity with you until I learn first this new separateness we have, the separateness that grows as you do. Remembering the Catholic woman talking of the Blessed Virgin's comfort, I decide to try it. *Emmelia,* I think, *help me. Monica, pray for me.* I wait for my help to come.

The parent-child separateness is what Pastor Nora learns from fostering. It is what I can learn from Joseph. Joseph's adoptive parenthood and Pastor Nora's fostering are both icons for what parenting is and should be. They are the icons I need right now as I find my way into our new separateness and new togetherness. I need them as my impulses for flourishing betray themselves, as my desire to keep you from disease causes me to inflict suffering on you. It is difficult to remain faithful to my better desires for you. It is so easy for me to betray them, and by them, to betray you as well. They need constant renewal, constant grace, constant divine enlivening. *Joseph, help me. Comfort Pastor Nora, Mother Mary. Protect baby Samantha.*

"Mommy?" Your voice interrupts my thoughts.

Looking up, I see you fidgeting in the doorway. I hold open

my arms, a gesture of invitation, or self-offering. *Hineni.* "You okay, sweetie?"

"I can't sleep." You are squinting in the light that seems so bright after the darkness of your bedroom. It is late, and we have plans early tomorrow. Normally, I would walk you down the hall and put you back to bed. I would calculate your lost sleep and how the morning might go. But tonight I listen to the worried note in your voice.

"Here, come sit by me." I make room on the couch, and you scoot beside me, laying your head on my lap as I smooth your hair. We snuggle for some moments in silence before you begin to shake with giggles.

"Mommy, can I crawl back into your belly?" I follow your gaze to a photograph of me heavily pregnant with you.

"I'm not sure you would fit anymore," I smile.

You are unconcerned with such practicalities. "It was so warm in there, Mommy, and so cozy, like a blanket." You are joking with me, delighted at your own humor. The stale nonsense of Jesus's words to Nicodemus comes to me afresh in your mischief. *You must be born again.*

"But it was probably a bit wet and dark, too, right?"

You shrug and laugh. The moment is light, but when it passes, Christ's words stay, heavy with presence. *How can anyone be born after having grown old?* The words swell within me, filling my thoughts, my heart, even, it seems, my body. You twitch, and I resume stroking your hair. I remember in Augustine's struggle with his libido, Lady Continence says, "Make the leap without anxiety; God will catch you and heal you." I am not sure how to leap, or what leap this moment requires. Can I take some small step that says yes to rebirth?

I reach for a vial of holy water—water from your baptismal font—and, thinking of Abraham and Isaac, Hannah and Samuel, Joseph and Jesus, Emmelia and Macrina, Monica and Augustine, and Pastor Nora and Samantha, bless us both. The water is cool and drips down our foreheads and noses. Is this rebirth? A quietness stills my spirit, and I feel more spacious, open maybe. My vision shifts, or my love ungrasps, and I know the gift of your separateness, how it is a way of returning love to me, how it moves both of us deeper into the source of all love. In this late-night caesura, I am a brighter, less weary version of myself, and my labor for you fills me with joy rather than fatigue. Shaded by my restfulness, you, too, relax. We sit wordlessly together as your eyelids grow heavy and you drift toward sleep. Even after I feel your body go limp, I stay with you, saying prayers over you before I carry you back to bed, both of us at peace.

CHAPTER 9

Communion

In the place where I had been angry with myself, within
my chamber where I felt the pang of penitence, where I
had made a sacrifice offering up my old life and placing
my hope in you as I first began to meditate on my renewal:
. . . there you gave gladness in my heart.

Over the next few weeks, I imagine you on the day of your First
Communion. In my vision, you proceed slowly toward the
front of the church, like a bride or a graduate, dressed in white, ap-
proaching the threshold of new life: new unity with Christ, faith newly
claimed as your own. In my daydream, you smile with excitement
and smooth your dress self-consciously, aware of yourself becoming
just a little more grown-up over the course of this ceremony. Your
father and I chose for you to be baptized, and in that ceremony, your
godparents' faith stood in for your own. But today is your choice,
your faith. You are taking your place in the Christian community
in a new way by making this ancient faith your own. Holding you
in my mind's eye, I hope you feel that lightness of being that I have
heard some saintly people feel in taking the Eucharist.

The imagined event, like so much in your life these days, underscores our separateness from one another. In it, you are participating in a Communion I cannot, leaving me in the pew as you enter more deeply into a Church that I remain on the margins of. Your journey to this moment is also separate from mine—a way of coming into your own pilgrimage life—as is your joy in reaching this event. I know I may be tempted to share your joy by giving you wonderful gifts, insinuating my presence into your happiness, blending myself into the joy of your Communion. But this temptation, as I have come to see it, springs from a diseased desire to possess you.

First Communion is its own joy, *your* own joy, directed toward the Christ whom you will receive as bread. It should not be about me or my desires. Over the last two years of religious education classes, you have been preparing for First Communion. For the last several weeks, you have been talking and dreaming about that day when you will enter a new intimacy with God that is wholly yours, even as it binds you to a community across time and space. In my vision, I discipline myself to be still and bask in the joy that glows from your eyes, your smile, your whole radiant body. My joy comes through quiet attunement to your own.

Of course, this reverie assumes you will actually take First Communion. I am not so sure you will. The first obstacle is this: before Communion, you have to make a confession. You, my beautiful, apology-refusing daughter, somehow have to sit alone with a priest and confess your sins to him. I cannot imagine you talking to a grown man alone, much less telling God a big "I'm sorry" through him. Everything about my experience with you these last eight years tells me you will not be able to do this, that this is beyond you.

If you, by some miracle, make it over the hurdle of confession, you must then somehow walk up in front of the whole church and receive Communion from a strange adult. Every week you have refused to go up for a blessing with your father as he takes the Eucharist. You cannot tolerate all the eyes looking at you as you approach the host; you resist the ritual movements of walking up, bowing, and crossing yourself that individuate each person at her moment before the Eucharistic minister. So every Mass you stay rooted to your seat, shaking your head and clutching the pew as we prod you to go forward with your father. How will you go up by yourself for the bread and wine on the day of First Communion? It seems impossible. But at the same time, I know you want to go. You have been talking about First Communion constantly. You want to know what the bread tastes like and what it feels like to eat it. You are excited and joyful (and worried). The actual date for the event is in one week, and the confessions are scheduled for tomorrow. Unsure what will happen, I have not bought you a dress.

I say a quick prayer for you, one of many I have offered for your First Communion, and turn back to my research. I am working on a book about Christian images, and today I am studying an icon of the Presentation of Jesus at the Temple. The structure of the scene is both strikingly simple and wonderfully complex. Four large figures dominate the scene. Mary is in the center. To her left are Joseph and the prophetess Anna. To her right, across an expanse of space, the holy man Simeon holds the Christ-child. The basic scene is easy to read: Mary and Simeon are the central pair, with Mary as a figure of loss, her hand still pointing toward the Christ-child, who reaches out to his mother from Simeon's arms. The other pair, Joseph and Anna, add to this central story. The presence of Joseph completes the Holy Family, and Anna carries a scroll announcing, "This child is the creator of the heavens and the earth." All four of them are in the Temple.

The longer I contemplate the icon, the more layers of meaning begin to emerge. These figures are not just inside a Temple

but standing before an altar. The babe Jesus—traditionally under-
stood to be forty days old, though he looks much older—rests in
Simeon's arms just above or before the altar. The placement suggests that the Christ-child is a gift, an offering. He is not the only
offering here. In Joseph's hands are two turtledoves, a fulfillment
of the injunction in Leviticus that forty days after the birth of the
firstborn son, the mother must bring a lamb and a turtledove to
the priest as a burnt offering. If the mother cannot afford a lamb,
the passage continues, she may bring two turtledoves. The two
turtledoves of the icon thus recall the humble background of the
Holy Family, and their placement in Joseph's hands communicates the way Joseph has taken his place in the family, carrying
the sacrifice on Mary's behalf.

These two sacrifices—of the doves and of Christ—help de-
pict the way Christ inaugurates a new age, one that transforms
Solomon's Temple into a Christian church. Another way this gets
displayed is through the four-pillared dome inside the Temple-
church. It is known as the *ciborium* and has a history in both Jew-
ish and Christian worship. In the Temple, the ciborium housed
the Ten Commandments and other contents of the tabernacle. It
was the holiest site, where the presence of God was manifest. In
the Catholic Church, the ciborium is usually quite small, an or-
nate vessel near the altar that houses the reserved host. When the
faithful enter the Catholic Church, they genuflect if the light near
the altar is on, indicating God's presence in the reserved bread
of the ciborium. But in those Orthodox Churches for which the
tradition of the ciborium survives, it looks more like it did in early
Christianity and in the icon: a canopy that covers the altar. In all
these cases, the ciborium marks and covers the presence of Christ
in the bread. In the icon of the Presentation at the Temple, the
ciborium is associated, not with Moses's stone tablets, but with a
gospel book just over it, and with the presence of the Christ-child.

So there is a shift from Temple to church ciborium. The stone tablets become a gospel book. The heavenly manna becomes the one who is the bread of heaven. These transformations suggest that Christ comes as the fulfillment of the law, as the realization of Israel's hope.

As the icon anticipates the church, so does it look toward the crucifixion, referencing the prophetic words of Simeon to Mary, "A sword will pierce through your own soul also." Father Maximos Constas points out the way the composition of the Presentation echoes that of the Crucifixion, with the altar replacing the Cross. His words about it are beautiful: "[T]he Presentation is portrayed as a complex matrix of love and loss. Mary's handing over of the child to Simeon, Simeon's desire to hold the child, the child's desire to be held (or his fear of such holding), and Simeon's plea to depart, die, to absent himself from the world (Lk 2:29), create a network of longing and desire so dense and complex as to be almost impossible to delineate. . . . In all of these images, Mary's loss of the child is central; first to Simeon and then to the cross." Mary's presentation of the Christ-babe at the Temple, like her losing the boy Christ at the Temple twelve years later, anticipates her loss of Christ on the cross. She offers Christ like a loaf of bread in the ciborium of the Presentation icon, and Christ becomes the bread of salvation on the cross years later.

The bread of the ciborium and altar is the bread we are preparing you to take at the end of the week. I think about Mary's gift of Christ, one that anticipates her loss of him to death, and wonder what that means for your father and me as we prepare for you to receive that bread, the communion bread that came from her loss. In sending you to the altar, I'm preparing you for a cruciform life, and, in some ways, for death. You take the Eucharist to become like the one who gave his life on the cross, the one who told us all to take up our cross and follow him. To take the

Eucharist is to reaffirm your baptismal promise to die to sin, to violence, and to un-love. So in First Communion, I am giving you up, sending you to receive Jesus, the child Mary gave for you and me and God and the Church. This moment foreshadows another moment when I will give you up in a new way, and my house will no longer be your home. It also foreshadows your death, and mine, as the union promised by the Eucharist is only consummated in death, when you will see Christ face to face. There is loss in this moment. But I also see how, in another sense, I cannot lose what I never possessed. You were never mine to claim. You were always my little stranger-kin, given to me for a time to love and cherish. If you are able to take your First Communion, we will enter more deeply into what we already are and into what Father Maximos calls the complex matrix of love and loss.

If is still the critical word. I wake the next morning, the day that your class has been assigned to make its confessions to the priest, with some anxiety. How will you do this? For your sake, I try to dispel my worry with a positive spirit. I want to feel peaceful and joyful about it. I want you to feel that peace and joy as well. You are not sure, at this point, what you will do. You say that you hope you will be able to confess, and later that day, just before dinner, you leave with your father to make a confession with the rest of the children in your class preparing for First Communion. Your father is, for reasons mysterious to me, more optimistic than I am, though I remain unbuoyed by his spirit.

As soon as you are gone, I allow myself to glower. I am frustrated by the bureaucracy of this process. I am angry that you have worked so hard to be ready for your First Communion and have become so excited about it—and now your anxiety may block your path to it. I have suggested that you might be able to write your confession rather than give it orally—or even that you might bring in a sheet of paper to read the confession in front of the priest. I have asked, too, if I can go in with you, or if your father can, to help you be more comfortable. All these requests have been denied. I have been close enough to the Catholic Church to see that neither utter theological illiteracy nor the feeblest commitment to the church prevents people from receiving the sacrament. Why can there be no accommodation made for you? Why can they not look beyond their bureaucratic apparatus and see a child who wants to encounter Christ in the bread of heaven?

I am working myself into a warmer anger now, fed by a sense of righteous indignation. My Protestant spirit of iconoclasm possesses me, and I want to sweep away all those mediations, all of those objects and rules that are supposed to help us draw nearer to Christ but so often just block us from the divine. It is the same iconoclastic spirit, I tell myself in this moment, of Jesus clearing the money changers out of the Temple; or telling the Pharisees that the Sabbath was made for people, not people for the Sabbath; or of Jesus eating, speaking, and associating with "inappropriate" people. It is surely the same spirit even of Pope Francis causing an uproar by washing the feet of a Muslim woman one Maundy Thursday. Pope Francis, I am certain of it now, would not approve of how your situation is being handled. After several minutes storming around the house alone, I have decided God is firmly on my side. Loving rules above a person constitutes the worst, most boring form of idolatry. I storm around some more, clattering dishes and stabbing vegetables as I angrily prepare our meal.

My anger peaks and, as I run out of vegetables to victimize, begins to subside. I see, I do, that I only care so much because the prize is so great. I see that unchecked, the iconoclastic spirit could go all the way to insisting that the Eucharist is one more mediation to be swept away. The Protestant impulse to take down all the guards around divine presence can work itself into a denial of divine presence. I acknowledge: I do not want all mediation, all rules, and all gifts to be swept away. I want there to be more consideration given to my particular child than our understaffed, underfunded church can manage when it is taking 300 children through First Communion with one priest and a few volunteers.

You are coming home now with your father. I cannot interpret your manner, which is neither upset nor happy. I look beyond you to your father, who shakes his head in response to my unasked question.

"What was it like?" I ask you with studied lightness.

"She was so close to making a confession," your father booms cheerily.

"I didn't do it," you protest.

Do your father and I acknowledge your disappointment before we spend the meal projecting as much positivity and hope as we can? I can't remember now. You finish eating and leave the table to lose yourself in a book.

I turn to your father, whose face relaxes into an expression of fatigue. "She kept thinking she could do it," he tells me. "She kept wanting to stay and try, but she just couldn't go and do it. Father Danilo has invited us to come back tomorrow and try again."

"Will things be any different then?" I try to keep my question neutral, but your father can hear my suppressed suspicion and accusation, traces of the Protestant spirit possessing me moments ago.

"Well, I don't know, but we'll try. There won't be other kids there this time." He speaks decisively. We wait for tomorrow.

When the time arrives the next day, you leave again for church with your father. Again I wait, this time more calmly, for you to return. I turn to my research to quell the temptation to anxiety. Today I am working on one of the icons of Christ's descent to the dead, the *Anastasis*. The image has special meaning for me. Its most famous version exists in a church I visited in Turkey days before learning of your presence in my womb. In it, Christ walks over the doors of Hades that he has broken down. The doors look to me like the grave covers in many icons, the iconographic version of the stone rolled away from the tomb. The icon announces that death has been conquered. Now Satan is chained, while the dead are freed, their chains broken, the keys and nails scattered about near the bottom of the icon. Christ reaches out to Adam and Eve, lifting them from the dwelling of the dead to the new life of resurrection.

I read one of my favorite theologians of icons, Paul Evdokimov, to see what he says about this image. He quotes Ephrem the Syrian's hymn on the descent, which imagines Christ saying to Adam as he descends, "Come to me my image and my likeness." Jesus speaks gently in Ephrem's imagining, like the good shepherd seeking his lost sheep or the widow seeking her lost coin. By contrast, Epiphanius, another theologian Evdokimov quotes, imagines Jesus arriving with more vigorous presence. He describes Jesus going to the dead and saying to Adam: "Get up out of the mass of dead people. I am your God and because of you, I have become your son." Epiphanius and Ephrem envision Jesus with very different demeanors, but I am also struck by the similarity of the scenes they describe. In particular, I notice that both picture a speaking Jesus. For them Jesus revivifies Adam and Eve the same way he created him: with words. I look back at the icon. It is an icon of such hope. Jesus is dressed in white and haloed by an additional white *mandorla* studded with stars. Set against the dark background, the luminous white suggests the light that conquers the darkness, the hope for all people.

Time passes quickly. You are back within the hour, your face and your father's jubilant. You are carrying ice cream. We break it open in celebration, and spoons in hands, go over the story, which seems to me like it ought to be included in a book of miracles of the twenty-first century.

This is your tale: You arrive at the church and head over to Father Danilo's office. Along the way, you run into Evie, a four-year-old that you help care for sometimes, looking after her in the cry room, helping her get her burritos in the after-Mass breakfast, and entertaining her after services. You like to take care of Evie because it gives you a clear social role, one focused on someone other than yourself. Evie's mom was just coming from confession as you were about to go in, and Evie spots you as they walk out of the office. She runs up to you and hugs you, delighted, and you play big sister to her, calling her sweetie and telling her what good hugs she gives.

Father Danilo watches this display of affection and, after a quick conference with Evie's mom, asks if you would like Evie to come in with you. Since she is not of canonical age, Father Danilo explains, Evie can be present for your confession. You smile shyly at him and nod. All four of you—your father, Father Danilo, Evie, and you—go into the office and share orange juice and animal crackers as Father Danilo attempts to chat with you but ends up speaking mostly with your father. He is gentle and warm. I remember at this point in the story that he has seven brothers and sisters back in the Philippines. He must have some nieces and nephews by now as well. I wonder if he misses them.

Soon after you finish the orange juice, it is time for your father to leave. The door closes, and your father watches through the window as Father Danilo asks a series of questions to which you either nod or shake your head. You speak no words, but you don't have to. It is enough to gesture and nod. Then it is over: your sins are forgiven; you are commanded to go and sin no more.

You are almost giddy by the time I see you. You seem so proud of yourself and happy. Leaning against me, you tease me that now you have two sacraments, baptism and confession, while I have just baptism. I retort with mock offense that I also have the sacrament of marriage, and so we have the same number. You grin, "Well, Mommy, after Saturday, I will have more than you." I smile and ruffle your hair. I hope that is true. We celebrate some more, and after you go to bed, your father tells me another part of the story: as you parted ways with Evie in the parking lot, you turned to give her a hug and, bending toward her, whispered, "I couldn't have done it without you, Evie."

The whole event seems to me marvelous, a wondrous clearing away of bureaucracy, or making a miraculous way through it, like the parting of the Red Sea that allows you to cross to a Promised Land of milk and honey and Eucharistic bread. It is a gift. But what will this mean for Saturday? Will you be able to endure the stares and perform the individual rituals in front of hundreds of congregants? It seems almost too much, at this point, to hope for another miracle, the miracle of your actually being able to go up and receive the Eucharist. But from another view, today's miracle seems to promise another. The greater difficulty is surmounted; surely the lesser won't stand in your way.

In my happiness, I tell your father how lucky we are that you made the confession given the Church's denial of our requests. He looks at me surprised. "They didn't deny our requests." Now I am surprised. He answers my expression, "I never made them because Father Danilo was committed to working something out for her. There's a whole First Communion class for children with disabilities, so of course the Church makes accommodations for children who can't do the standard communion prep." For a moment, I am confounded. How is his story so different from mine? Haven't we been suffering this drama together? Or have I been in a completely different story than your father? Disoriented, I feel again my outsider status to this Church you are entering more deeply. But as the image of you coming home this evening, exuberant and joking, returns to me, joy swallows my confusion and estrangement. Perhaps others have been more committed to you than I knew. Isn't that cause for more happiness rather than less? Shouldn't it lighten my load to have co-laborers bearing the weight of your spiritual health? I decide that it should and go to sleep in deep gratitude to Father Danilo, to Evie, to your father, to God. I feel as if a burden has been rolled away. Eyes closed, body still in my dark room, I am at peace.

I wake in the night with a start. I have been dreaming, but I can't recall what the dream was. In the foggy thought of half-wakefulness, an image floats in my mind. It is the *Anastasis*. As it comes into view of my mind's eye, a voice like a loud roar of wind, rushes up from my memory: "Get up out of the mass of dead people. I am your God and because of you, I have become your son." That is what woke me—those roaring words of Epiphanius I had read earlier that afternoon, replayed in a dream. But no, I think, as my mind begins to clear. Those weren't exactly the words of my dream. The voice had said, *Get up out of that mass of death.* The words seem spoken directly to my spirit. *I am your God and because of you, I have become yours.*

What does it mean? *Does* it mean anything? In Epiphanius's homily, Jesus says these words to Adam, who had, by his sin, fallen into a mass of death. To rescue him, God becomes human, a son of Adam, and pulls Adam into a new life that sin and death cannot corrupt. What are these words for me? *I am your God and because of you, I have become yours.* Is the "yours" a stand-in for "your daughter?" It could as easily be "your mother" or "your savior." But I have long thought that you are like the Messiah to me, that divine grace comes to me in your presence, in both what is wonderful and what is difficult about it for me. God saved Adam by becoming his child. Are you, my own child, how God is saving me? My life with you has exposed me, my sinfulness, and my death. You have given me the grace of a more open-eyed vision of myself. And life with you has given me new capacities for love, mercy, and courage. By you, I am learning again the vulnerability and playfulness of childhood. Your life has made me more alive— more, I hope, like Life, like divine life.

You are one of those mediations of God in my life. You bear God to me, make God present to me. Because you are an image of the Messiah to me, to address myself to you is, indirectly, to address myself to the divine, to the way that divine life is making its way in me, the way I am striving with divine powers, receiving wounding and blessing. To address you and my loving struggle to help you give birth to your own free will is also to address myself to the God in whose likeness I long to be reborn. God has come to me in you to draw me out of death.

There is more here. Christ becomes his son Adam's son. In a different way, Emmelia becomes her daughter Macrina's daughter. This is what we must be willing to do for our children: to become their children. I must—I tell myself once again—be willing to become my daughter's daughter. The physical world witnesses to this spiritual reality. As we age, we all become our daughters' daughters. As we lose the ability to care for ourselves, we must yield to the care of our children. This is no less true in the spiritual world. As our children grow into spiritual maturity—even before they arrive—we must be willing to become their sons and daughters. On one point, though, the spiritual truth of this reversal differs from the biological one: we become our children's children by their physical care because of our own biological failings; but in the spiritual world, it is not out of our weakness so much as their strength. (Adam, of course, is a more complex case; it is both his weakness and his strength. Christ's coming both exposes the depth of Adam's sin and reveals the glory in his position as the first human.)

One way to describe this willingness to become one's daughter's daughter is as part of our movement from strangers to friends.

When you lived in my womb, we were, in some ways, closer than we have ever been, or ever will be. We were so close that we shared my body. We were so close that we could not be friends. After all, you were just a little piece of me, a part of me. One cannot be friends with one's limbs. But the more separate you have become—and the more I accept your separateness—the more we move toward real friendship with one another. My acknowledgment of you as a distinct person is the condition for the freedom we need for true friendship to take root. My willingness to become your daughter names the equality requisite for full friendship to blossom.

It will be some time before we achieve this equality and freedom, but we are on our way. I am learning to respect you in new ways and to trust in the divine grace at work in you. I am also aware of the possibility of failure and of the importance of relinquishing the illusion I can avoid failure for you. I want the best for you, daughter, but I cannot will the best for you. I am learning to make space for your own will to grow. All that said, my little friend, I still don't know if you will go forward on Saturday.

I return to sleep with no further dreams or visions, and the rest of the week passes busily. We buy your Communion dress, order a cake, and make other little preparations as our house grows full of grandparents in town for the occasion. We have made alternate plans to celebrate Saturday as "the possibility of First Communion" if you cannot go up. At last the day arrives. In the morning, the house brims with nervous enthusiasm. Your father takes you to the church early to rehearse with the other communicants. I arrive later, with those who have come to share in the joy of this day. I am thinking of what last words I will say to you, what charge I can give you that will fill you with life and hope. If words fail me, at least I can give you a good hug. I want you to know how happy I am for you, how happy I will be whatever happens today.

Pulling into the parking lot, I am surprised how many cars are already there, twenty minutes before Mass is scheduled to begin. I park and get out, but before I can go around to the line of First Communicants at the front of the church, your father hails me at the side entrance. Mass, he tells me, is beginning. You have already filed inside with all the other First Communicants. Seeing my consternation, your father places a hand on my arm. "They changed the time and forgot to tell our class," he tells me. "I have some seats for us in here."

My spirit of protest is ready to possess me, but I resist its seductions. Now is not the time for fighting and protesting; it is the time for presence. I want to absorb the occasion, to imprint the day on my memory and remind you about it someday. I see so many excited eight-year-olds. The girls especially stand out. With their veils and stiff, lacy dresses, many of them look like brides, as I imagined you would. But I easily pick you out from among them because you do not look like a bride—not a traditional one, at least. You wear a simple white dress that hangs down rather than blousing out. You chose it because it isn't fussy and doesn't, you think, draw too much attention to yourself.

You are many pews up from us in the crowded church, but I keep my eye on you, trying to discern how you are doing, what you are feeling. You are on the very end of your pew, in the seat nearest to where Father Danilo will stand when he administers the Eucharist. "Is she sitting there because . . . ?" I whisper to your father, who nods. "They thought it would be easier for her if she only had to walk a couple steps." I hope they are right. I can see it going both ways, for there is another side to this seating arrangement. It means you will have to be the first of the communicants to receive.

The readings and homily pass quickly. Soon the priest is consecrating the host. It is almost time for you to stand. You are so beautiful, and I am filled with love for you. I want you to move toward what you desire. I want you to be free. I know your freedom is a gift I cannot give you.

Now it is time. The communion music plays softly, and all the children in your row stand up. I see Father Danilo smile at you and nod encouragement. You take a sideways step out of your pew and pause, as if frozen. The priest is so close, just a couple steps away. I sit and pray for you to go up. I cannot tell: Are you moving or have you stopped? It is difficult to say. I fix my eyes on your white dress and watch with hope.

PART II

To My God

CHAPTER 10

Memory

This power of memory is great, very great, my God. It is a
vast and infinite profundity. Who has plumbed its bottom?

I turn my attention now to You—You who comes to me in the
one I birthed, You who births me to new life.

But where was my attention before, if it wasn't with You?
When I consider my life with my child, aren't You there, revealing Yourself in my meditations? When I discover sources of renewal and grace, whose are they if not Yours? When in fury or
pride, I betray my love for my daughter, don't I also betray You?
And when I am reborn into a better love, isn't it in Your womb?

Again and again, I discover You coming to me in my life with
my daughter. She has always been for me an image of You. But
now I turn myself to You in a different way. Now I address You
directly—as directly as a creature can address her Creator.

I have been wandering through the fields and palaces of memory, discovering what it means to be converted and to assist another's conversion. I have been exploring birth and rebirth in these
memory journeys and finding You in these quests. But what does

it mean to find You in my memory? Augustine writes that You are not present in his memory until he learns of You. Surely he means, though, that learning of You makes You present as an explicit concept. In so much of Augustine's narration of his memories, he notes a divine presence he can perceive only in retrospect. In the moment of first experiencing the event, You were obscure to him, but no less present. You were with him, as Augustine writes, but he was not with You. Then in memory, he experiences the event again, with an awareness of Your presence to him. When Augustine remembers his life, he remembers You, even though his past self failed to recognize Your presence in his life. By his memory, Augustine discovers that his life opens up to reveal Your own; through memory, he meets You the Creator, Sustainer, and Redeemer. He remembers, and he finds himself in the story of Your life with the world. You—in Your resonant, resplendent, fragrant, mouth-watering, enflaming presence—enliven him to perceive You. Awake, he can see You are everywhere in his life, everywhere in his memory, everywhere in the world.

I searched for You in my own memory in an effort to seek You in the world. But what kind of attempt is this? Where in the world is memory? Where am I when I journey through my memory? When I am absorbed in memory, the past becomes present to me in a different way. I relive the sights, sounds, smells, tastes, and emotions of events that are removed from my present self. Even though my senses give me the impressions I store in memory, recollection is not exactly a sensory exercise. I could lose my sense of smell and still recall a scent. Alone, at my desk at night, I remember my child as a baby, as she was at just three months old, as I held her one sunny day—her milky exhales, her gurgles like cat purrs, her eyes peering into my own. I traced my finger around the features of her face as her eyes widened in wonder at the sensation. Now while I remember this moment with my baby, it and she are more alive to me than my surroundings. Where am I as I remember—with my baby or at my desk?

As Augustine points out, there is no physical baby in my mind, nor a literal sunny day, for objects themselves are not present in our memory; rather, images of those objects are present to us when we recall them. When I remember my child as a baby, she is present to me in a particular way through this image of her, sometimes vividly, sometimes faintly. In a way, the image gives my child to me. And through the image of my child, my memory also gives to me images of You. It is a series of mediations: My child, who is given to me as an image in my memory, is often also an image of You, the God who comes to me in Jesus. So in my memory, I find an image of my child who is an image of You; You are in the vast fields and palaces of my memory. You are present to me—to all of us—through memory. I imagine Mary intuitively knew this, pondering and treasuring, as she did, Your infancy in her heart, receiving each little moment like a jewel to be stored within, retrieving those jewels to wonder at them anew as Your childhood passed quickly into adulthood.

The Church has practiced many different ways of receiving the presences of memory. Good Friday performances of the live stations of the cross replay the events of Christ's crucifixion. Pilgrimages through the Holy Land retell Your earthly life in the places where You once walked. Prayerful meditations like the Ignatian exercises enjoin the contemplative to use her imagination to enter into the mystery of the gospel. Even the liturgy is an exercise in memory and imagination to awaken the faithful to the reality of Your life— and to yield Your presence to them. All of these practices draw on an understanding of memory as more than a sign pointing to a distant signified. These practices are not supposed to yield simply cognitive renewal, for they do not give mere knowledge. They give a presence that potentially renews, even transforms the whole person. The power of memory is great.

What is this powerful memory? Augustine imagines memory, not only like fields and palaces, but also like a cave of wonders. It is, he writes, a "huge cavern, with its mysterious, secret, and indescribable nooks and crannies." Each perception enters by its own gate and is "put on deposit there." There is something about that description of memories as like cave deposits that strikes me as apt. Often memories are described as if they are like other deposits, bank deposits, where one puts in one hundred dollars and can withdraw at will that same one hundred dollars, unchanged. But a cave deposit models the way memories constantly, often imperceptibly, change. They build up into stalactites and stalagmites that support certain narratives; they are altered when recalled into the light of consciousness. Each turning over of a memory in my mind brings modifications, losses, and accretions. Sometimes the change can be quite radical, as when whole episodes are created and stored in the memory. I recently read a story about people who had been coerced into confessing a murder, were then exonerated years later, and could not come to terms with that exoneration, convinced as they were of the false memories of murder that had consolidated over the years. As I remember my baby, sometimes I may create memories of events that others tell me never happened, perhaps especially regarding those moments I think about and describe often to others.

Isn't this what the Church has done in remembering the ones it loves? In the early years of Christianity, some of those who loved You tried to imagine Your infancy and childhood. While the gospels regularly read in Christian worship—the gospels later declared part of the canon of Scripture—said very little about You as a baby or boy, other texts written by early Christians describe You performing amazing feats as a youth. In the stories recorded in the

Infancy Gospel of Thomas, You miraculously lengthen a beam of wood for Your father. You make clay sparrows and then bring them to life. You strike dead a boy who hits Your shoulder. To me, the stories read like a fanciful attempt to reconcile the reality of boyhood, and all its impulsiveness and petulance, with the reality that You are also the all-powerful creator of the universe.

Those boyhood stories of Jesus never became central to Christian proclamation or study. The case is different for the stories of Mary. As the Church grew in love for her, Christians also imagined what Mary's childhood was like and who her parents were, especially in a second-century document called the Protoevangelium of James. The stories in the Protoevangelium of James made their way into the memory of the Church, even as the book itself was never canonized. Because of its tales, the Church recognizes Mary's parents as named Anna and Joachim; it has given them feast days, special prayers, and icons. These stories, which became encoded in tradition, were not just written down decades after Mary lived; they were perhaps made up decades after Mary lived. I have a hard time reckoning them historical records myself. And if they are not historical, what kind of reality do they have for us now? Are You there in those stories? When the Church finds these stories in its memory, what has it found? "This power of memory is great, very great, my God. It is a vast and infinite profundity. Who has plumbed its bottom?" Are these examples or betrayals of the power of memory?

If Anna and Joachim may not be historical persons, then how is their reality different from that of Antigone, Merida, or Hermione Granger? What am I doing when I contemplate the image of holy people who may have no historical existence? I do not contemplate *nothing*. Anna and Joachim emerge from the faithful's loving devotion to Mary; they pass through the piety of many souls over the centuries as their stories are filled out and refined.

In contemplating Anna and Joachim, am I learning how holy people have contemplated Mary, herself a person who helps us contemplate You? In praying with Anna and Joachim, do I wander through images created through, by, and for the contemplation of holy people, images that have spoken to them of You and Your revelation in Scripture? Fashioned and honed by the prayers of saints, might these figures become images of the divine? Their making is not dissimilar from the making of icons—born of the collective imagination of the Church, hallowed by the prayers of the faithful. Perhaps by such making, memory becomes a site of sacred images, a place to meet You.

Years ago, I climbed Mount Sinai, silently praying the Psalms pilgrims have prayed ascending Sinai for centuries. I had just visited the nearby monastery where I met with monks and saw the ancient icons. I did this as a graduate student, knowing that there is doubt about the location of Sinai and even whether the Sinai story ever historically transpired. I have wondered many times since what exactly I was doing as I climbed up that mountain, aware of its dubious history. Was my climb in my memory—in my prayers, in my desires—unrelated to my physical climb up a particular mountain? That cannot be right. It is not as if that mountain were interchangeable with any other. Why would I go to Egypt if it were? There was something about the earth on that mountain, that particular place that Christians have been calling Sinai for centuries. Could so much prayer leave a place untouched? Or might those prayers have transfigured the earth on that mountain? Some people correlate Sinai with Tabor, and so claim that in Your human life, You Yourself treat Sinai as sacred, climbing up that mountain under the name Tabor for Your own Transfiguration. According to such traditions, on that mount of doubtful historicity, You show Your glory and then descend to minister to the people You love. They cry, "Lord, have mercy!"

It strikes me as significant that Your journey on Tabor ends with a descent in mercy and renewed attention to the suffering, need, and sickness of earthly life. False dramas float away from the earth, puffing us up with the airiness of their nonexistence. But the Sinai of the Church's imagination becomes Tabor, a mountain that does not lead us into clouds that obscure the world but takes us down to the people You love, down to acts of mercy. Where do Anna and Joachim take us? One hopes they take us into greater faithfulness, into more loving parenthood, into a life of receiving and giving great gifts, gifts like Mary, Mother of God.

There are other stories and figures that I find in my memory by way of the Church's collective memory. Some of these stories do not seem to me divine images. At least, they seem to image the divine in a very imperfect, damaged way. One of these is the story of St. Catherine of Alexandria, a saint whose story bothers me twice-over. According to legend, she was an intelligent, beautiful, and well-educated woman who rebuked the emperor for persecuting Christians, defeated the arguments of his most learned scholars, and by her eloquence persuaded some scholars to become Christians. When the emperor could not conquer her by argument, he attempted to subdue her by marriage, which she refused. For her unyielding courage and inspiring intellect, she was tortured on a wheel, which consequently broke into pieces and killed, in many versions of the story, a crowd of thousands cheering her torture. I hate that story of a God who repays violence with greater violence and reveals divine power through killing. But the still grimmer level to that story is that St. Catherine's tale is rooted in a historical event where Christians, not pagans, were the persecutors. The legend of Catherine cloaks the violence Christians did to the pagan woman Hypatia, a well-regarded teacher of philosophy and astronomy in Alexandria. The head of the Neoplatonist school in Alexandria, Hypatia was murdered

by a mob because it blamed her, in some accounts, for the failure
of two church officials to reconcile with one another. The Christians dragged her from her carriage, took her to a church, and
stripped her. In one account, they then "murdered her with tiles.
After tearing her body to pieces, they took her mangled limbs
to a place called Cinaron, and there burnt them." Another tells a
similar story, where the Christians "tare [*sic*] off her clothing and
dragged her . . . through the streets of the city till she died. And
they carried her to a place called Cinaron, and they burned her
body with fire." The account of violence is disturbingly similar to
the lynching of Jesse Washington.

What do I, knowing this, make of the story, images, and figure
of St. Catherine of Alexandria, patron saint of libraries, girls, and
theologians? Do I strive to stamp this image out of the Church's
collective memory, to excise it by repression? Or do I keep taking that memory out, retelling it through the story of Hypatia,
restoring to the Church's memory this tale's jagged edges, helping to make it a memory where You, God, can be found? How
can I find You in this story of the Church's memory? How can
I repair that memory to help others meet You in the story? Can
the figure of Catherine-Hypatia become a way of exposing our
own violence and anti-Christ tendencies? Can she call us to re-
pentance, to greater fidelity to You?

I hope she can. I hope the Church can learn to name Your
presence in its memory of Catherine and Hypatia, as I am learning to name Your presence even in my more painful memories of
life with my daughter. I have learned to meet You in my daughter's
neediness, in her resistance to my desires, and in her separateness
from me. I discover You, not only in the wide-eyed wonder of the
babe looking at me in love that sunny day, but also in the infant
hungry for milk, in the child whose desires deviate from my own,
and in the daughter I attempt to dominate. Maybe the Church

can, in a similar vein, discern Your presence in Hypatia's teacherly wisdom it found so threatening, in her horrific persecution at its hands, in her innocence of the charges leveled against her. Maybe the Church rightly remembers Hypatia by recognizing itself as one that crucifies the wise, good, and innocent, by learning again the lesson that we are the betrayers of Christ. It is a more distressing, though not a fundamentally different, exercise than what the faithful do with so many of the saints. They have learned to follow the tortuous passageways of memory to find the excesses hidden there. They know, after all, how to meet You in the sacrifice of Anna and in both the motherhood and the daughterhood of her daughter Mary, the one we call the Mother of God, even as You remain Mother of us all—Mary, Anna, Hypatia, my daughter, and me.

See how widely I have ranged, Lord, searching for You in my memory. Teach me to seek You rightly, to find You in my memory, to learn mercifulness through my memory of my daughter and of those the Church has named as saints. May I receive the images of memory and help fashion the Church's imagination as conduits of Your divine presence. May I learn through these images to find You and love You better. For, always late have I loved You, Beauty so ancient and so new. In the ancient, may I find Your presence, ever-new. In the new, may I find You in whom all time exists. May I learn to love You better by finding You who are beyond time in all the time You give us—and in all our struggles to remember that time in love and faithfulness. And in this way, may I, my Mother God, grow to know You as You know me.

CHAPTER 11

Eternity

*It is not in time that you precede time. Otherwise you
would not precede all times. In the sublimity of an eternity
which is always in the present, you are before all things
past and transcend all things future.*

On the desk, my icon of You as the Christ-child held by the
Madonna sits beside a photograph of my daughter as an
infant. They are a curious pairing. In this icon of the Christ-child,
You look more like a small adult than like an infant. You reach
for Your mother's head-covering with the playful affection of a
child and the wise eyes and winnowed limbs of one much older.
Like Your mother, You are flat in this image, represented without
perspective, and haloed in gold.

My daughter has no halo. The light filtering in from the window dapples her skin and emphasizes her three-dimensionality.
Her full, chubby body is proportioned like a baby's rather than
an adult's: her eyes so large for her face, her face so large for her
body, her belly so large for her limbs. Her body twists against my
arm, leaning toward the camera with a mischievous grin. Her
tongue reaches for her chin.

Even though my eight-year-old daughter sleeps in the next room, I long for this little baby in the photograph before me, the baby she once was. What has happened to her? Is she lost to me? Or is she somehow still present to me in the growing girl I am raising? What happens to all of our successive selves that exist in time? Which one, to put the question as an old theological conundrum, is raised to new life in the resurrection of the dead and the life of the world to come? Are they all raised, such that we meet thousands of different versions of ourselves, from infancy to childhood to adolescence through each stage of adulthood? Or is only one self raised? Augustine mused once that we would be raised around the age of thirty-three, before the bloom of youth has entirely faded. But what would happen to all the other selves? Would they dissipate into nothingness?

As I long for my infant daughter, I also long for my own past self, a young mother full of wonder at the new capacities of her body. Pregnancy and nursing were difficult and inconvenient, but they also pressed me into a new relationship with my fleshly self. Now my body feels less powerful, less relevant. It nurtures no life, not biologically and directly, anyway. What were once sites of new capacities have melted into flabbier, weaker, more scarred witnesses to that one-time power. Only my arms, holding a child growing ever-larger over the years, are stronger. On the whole, my body bends toward death.

I miss other past selves, too. At times, I wish for the intensity of my twenties, as the world kept opening before me, showing me new sides of itself, surprising me with its depth and complexity. As the world grew, I grew, and I thrilled with my own vitality. I plunged from exuberance at new loves and possibilities to despair at loss and injustice. The mysteriousness of an individual person, the countless paths before me, the sheer enormity of life, agitated and exhilarated me. My passions now have less rein. I am calmer, milder, more centered, and this, too, feels like a precursor to death.

My longing for my daughter is coupled with this longing for my lost selves; it insinuates a longing for a self that is without loss, a self that might contain all other selves. As I look at the photograph of her in my arms, my infant babe is so real to me and yet so absent, even as my daughter lives. I think of Ted Hughes's poem "Six Young Men," in which Hughes mulls over an image of six military men in World War I who were all dead within six months of the photograph. The poem lingers over their vitality expressed in the photograph, which confounds the fact of their death. Hughes tries to hold in view both their liveliness and their deadness as he gazes at the men's likenesses. His last stanza performs his confounding. The men are demonstrably alive: "That man's not more alive whom you confront / And shake by the hand, see hale, hear speak loud, / Than any of these six celluloid smiles are." And the men are undeniably dead: "Nor prehistoric or, fabulous beast more dead." Their deadness, in fact, is so real as to have its own vitalness: "No thought so vivid as their smoking-blood." Hughes concludes as these confounding thoughts lead him into horror: "To regard this photograph might well dement, / Such contradictory permanent horrors here / Smile from the single exposure and shoulder out / One's own body from its instant and heat."

Hughes's poem speaks particularly to the terrors of war and mortality, but it suggests a horror that extends beyond them, to the simultaneous realities of death and vitality. His encounter with that photograph also speaks to a broader bewilderment about where the past is in relation to the present, to a shock at the loss of all past selves smiling in photographs. Photographs, after all, register the past, not the present. They are records of loss. Even selfies of present delight—eating food, enjoying friends, walking on the beach—even ones instantly uploaded and shared, record the loss of absorption that the photograph is meant to present. A person sharing a photo of himself frolicking on the beach is no longer frolicking on the beach, nor is the person uploading a romantic moment with a significant other any longer overpowered by the force of that moment. And the photograph of my baby shows me the daughter who is no longer mine to care for. Though the same person, she is also a different kind of daughter, an older one, whom I do not nurse, do not rock, do not buckle into baby carriers.

What is different about this icon of You with Your mother, which does not inspire such melancholy? It inspires devotion, joy, sometimes sadness of knowing the suffering the mother and child are destined for. But there is no sadness of loss, no lament for a bygone person or time. What is different about these images? Evdokimov, convinced of the categorical superiority of icons, describes the difference in terms of how icons and other human-made images work. For him, noniconic images like photographs provoke remembrance, while icons present the person in a new way. The photograph presents a moment in time and takes the memory back to that moment. But eternity calls to the beholder of the icon, inviting her to participate more fully in it, summoning her through the icon as if through a gate.

If the two images offer different types of presence, they must also trace different absences. Even as the icon gives Your personal presence, it also reminds the viewer that You are not present in the way You once were, when You walked on this earth as a human, nor in the way You one day will be, when You will fill the earth, Your presence all in all. But in the icon's invitation to eternity, it promises this future presence and gives the beholder a taste of it. Even the absence the icon traces promises future presence. The photograph makes no such promises. It only testifies to what once was, a moment that cannot be recaptured. The presence it yields is anemic compared to what the icon offers.

When I devote myself to an icon of a saint in prayer, the saint becomes present to me. She journeys to me, uniting to her likeness, extending blessing and interceding for my petitions. The person in the photograph makes no such journey. Her resemblance is there, and I can find that person again in my memory and make her live in my imagination. I can remember the feel of my daughter's infant skin, thin, warm, and soft as down. But her person does not come to me from the photograph, and so the photograph seems to speak of loss. The great German picture theorist Hans Belting wrote once that the origins of images were in death masks; we first made pictures to remember the dead, those who were no longer with us. The presence those death images gave at the same time announced a much more powerful absence.

It might seem as if photographs foreground absence, icons presence; photographs time, icons eternity. But this way of putting it, as one of strong contrasts between eternity and time, presence and absence, icon and photograph, cannot be right. Time does not exist in opposition to eternity but within it and by it—by You, the Eternal One. As Augustine asks, "What times existed which were not brought into being by you?" Eternity is not what comes before and after time, as if the two are in a struggle in which time currently has the upper hand. There is no such thing as "before" time, for "You have made time itself. Time could not elapse before you made time." Time exists within eternity, sustained by it. In opposing it, time only opposes itself.

To claim that time cannot be pit against eternity, to assert that eternity contains all time, is to affirm that loss does not have the final say for Christians. What could this mean? Augustine's idea that we will be raised at the age of thirty-three suggests a way that we as individuals will not suffer any loss to our personal gifts; we will be raised at the maximum of our powers, strength, and beauty. But as a community, absence emerges in a different way. Even if we were able to capture the wisdom of old age in our thirty-three-year-old bodies, we would have no children or babies in our raised community. And what a great loss, to have only adult bodies loving and praising You! We would miss children; perhaps I would even miss myself as a child. Can the entrance into eternity mean the erasure of childhood? I cannot imagine that You who told us we must enter the kingdom like little children would banish childhood from that kingdom. The end of childhood seems another way of making time the enemy of eternity.

Gregory of Nyssa, Macrina's younger brother, imagined our resurrection as one in which every hair from our head, all those hairs lost to baldness and brushing and illness, would be restored. He lived, of course, long before the knowledge we have today of exactly how much hair we produce in a lifetime, but I like his attempt to imagine a world without loss. He, too, however, came up against the limits of his imagination. He wonders what the resurrection means for those born unable to walk, for example. Would they be raised with legs that can walk? Would the blind be raised with sight? The deaf with hearing? On the one hand, they must, according to Gregory's logic. If our wounds and incapacities are not healed, then what kind of hope is the resurrection? At the same time, if the blind person is raised as a sighted one, how is it the same person who is raised? Is there not some loss to identity? Gregory raises but does not resolve this dilemma.

There is a similar problem with our childhood and adulthood; our identity extends throughout time, and to raise us at the height of our powers, would seem to shave off different parts of our identity. And this cannot be the way of the Eternal One, You who "created all times and exist before all times." "Your 'years,'" Augustine writes, "neither go nor come. Ours come and go so that all may come in succession. All your 'years' subsist in simultaneity because they do not change; those going away are not thrust out by those coming in. But the years which are ours will not all be until all years have ceased to be. Your 'years' are 'one day,' and your 'day' is not any and every day but Today, because your Today does not yield to tomorrow, nor did it follow a yesterday. Your Today is eternity." Augustine's hymn to You envisions Your presence containing and gathering all years together because You are eternal. Perhaps this is some clue of what we may hope for.

The experience of looking at a photograph might suggest something of how time may be integrated, or at least how the past and present are complexly interwoven. As a child of the fourth century, Augustine had no photographs, but he did have memory images. He writes of them, "Thus, my boyhood, which is no longer, lies in past time which is no longer. But when I am recollecting and telling my story, I am looking on its image in present time, since it is still in my memory." That his boyhood continues to exist as an image in his memory gives the past a vitality. However, it is not a vitality that shoulders Augustine out of the ordinary. "Who can deny that the past does not now exist? Yet there is still in the mind a memory of the past. None can deny that present time lacks any extension because it passes in a flash. Yet attention is continuous, and it is through this that what will be present progresses towards being absent." Attending to photographs and memory images gives the past moment a duration in the present, even as the present moment tends toward its own absence. Looking at photographs of my past makes me, in the moment of my attention, a self that contains my past self in some way—one of my past selves, at least. It is perhaps a hint of the world to come, a foretaste of a self and world without loss.

I cannot unriddle this way of hoping for a time that resolves in eternity. With Augustine, I confess that I still do not know what

time is, even as I know myself to be conditioned by it. But perhaps the photograph of my child, like the icon of You, murmurs
guidance. I look at my child in the photograph, this moment of
time when her growing body presses against mine. Her eyes are
large and happy as she reaches outward. Opened wide, her eyes
gaze at the world without defense or armor. In her openness and
vulnerability, in the way she calls my past into my present, I brush
against Your eternity.

CHAPTER 12

Materiality

You were, the rest was nothing. Out of nothing you made heaven and earth, two entities, one close to you, the other close to being nothing; the one to which only you are superior, the other to which what is inferior is nothingness.

Augustine likes to emphasize the difference between You and creation, and between the immaterial and the material. But doesn't the first difference chasten the second? You are so different from creation that the difference between the heavens and the earth is as nothing before You. The heavens are, Augustine writes, "derived from you, our God, but in such a way as to be wholly other than you and not Being itself." You are so different from creation, in fact, that You transcend any difference with it. You are present to creation without being any less God by that presence. You are present to the lowest part of the earth, breathing it into life, without ceasing to be God. And You are always giving more of Yourself to creation, You who joined with creation in the incarnation, You who seek to draw all creation into Your Triune life. You are *always and in all things seeking to realize the mystery of Your embodiment.*

The phrase is not mine. It's Paul Blowers's translation of seventh-century monk Maximus the Confessor, famous for his reflections on love and the cosmic dimensions of Christ. The words stay with me, sinking into my imagination of who You are—*the mystery of Your embodiment.* The phrase describes Your incarnation as a human, not as an afterthought to Your identity as God, like a garment You learned to put on for a time, but as revealing something deep about You, about who You eternally are. The mystery of embodiment is part of Your identity, and You, Incarnate One, ceaselessly seek to realize it, embodying Yourself in the bread and wine, in the Church, in the saint, in the priest, in the least of these, in the two or three gathered in Your name. Always and everywhere You seek to realize the mystery of Your embodiment.

The phrase communicates the intimacy of You to Your creation. It is not that creation is simply a staging ground for the incarnation, nor a screen for projecting Your divine works. Creation is part of this mysterious embodiment-seeking of You, Incarnate One, Word, *Logos.* I could narrate You this way: In creation, as in and because of the incarnation, the Logos seeks to realize the mystery of Her embodiment. She who bodies forth in the incarnation bodies forth in creation. By creation, She embodies Herself by giving Her own divine presence to sustain a presence different from Herself, the world. By incarnation, She embodies Herself by giving divine personhood to a human nature and so to humanity and so to the world. Both creation and incarnation reveal the purposes and character of God: for God so loved the world. In this way, the ends and modes of creation and incarnation are bound together.

For Maximus, the ways You seek to realize the mystery of Your embodiment reveal Your playfulness. He quotes from Gregory of Nazianzus, "For the divine one on high plays in all sorts of forms / Mingling with the world here and there / Following divine desires." You realize the mystery of Your embodiment, Lord, not like a person of business or politics pursuing a vision, at the expense of all else. You realize it like a child, playing with different forms, appearing in one location and another in a game of cosmic hide and seek. You follow Your desires into the world, and in Your playful appearing, You elicit our own desire, so that we, like delighted children, will chase after You. You are the eternally young God, who calls to us like a child, that we may become like children.

Your childhood is different from our own, natural childhood. You are not a child out of ignorance, inexperience, or naïveté. It is not that You are unfamiliar with sorrow or unacquainted with grief, nor do You fail to share the heavy burdens of a world filled with peril, suffering, and hardship. Your childhood is open-eyed in a way different from our first childhood. You in Your childhood know all the sorrow and violence of the world but remain open, vulnerable, and delighted by the good. G. K. Chesterton imagines You like a child who loves a good trick and so says, over and over, "Again, again, again!" to every sunrise. By Your untiring pleasure, the world goes on. The sun dawns with Your delight again and again.

Again and again. How many times have I heard that from my own child? How often have I witnessed her endless joy at the way her father flips her feet over her head, her never-satiated appetite for tickle time, her persistent cajoling me to make a funny face once more? My habit is to commiserate with other parents as we express amused exasperation with this thirst for repetition and remark at what funny little creatures children are, as we congratulate ourselves for tolerating their antics. I think it is a way that we assure ourselves that we adults are the normal ones and that a mild annoyance over certain childish behaviors is ordinary and forgivable.

But what if we have it backwards? What if these encounters with children who desire repetition reveal, not an odd feature of

children, but an odd feature of adults? What if, that is, children have
the normal response to delight, and adults have forgotten it, or can
no longer tolerate extended delight? What if, in the cosmic scheme
of things, it is our annoyance, not their "again," that is strange?
How do we journey out of our own world-weariness, disappointment, despair, and violence to the abundant life of peace?
Isaiah claims that a little child shall lead them. The passage's
pleasing ambiguity invites multiple interpretations. You, the Most
High God, lead us like a little child, as with Your game of cosmic hide and seek. Then also, the little children around us lead
by, among other ways, inviting us into their delightedness at the
world. And finally, You came to us as a little child to lead us when
You came in the incarnation. You came as an infinitesimal zygote,
a gift in response to Mary's yes. Little Child, lead us into Your
joy. Take us into Your peaceful kingdom, where even the wolf lies
down with the lamb.

I am learning to pray to You, the Child who saves us. One who
helps me in my lessons is Ephrem the Syrian, who wrote beautiful
hymns on the incarnation and Your childhood. In one, he writes:

Have mercy, O Lord, on my children!
In my children,
Call to mind Thy childhood,
Thou who wast a child.
Let them that are like Thy childhood
Be saved by Thy grace.

Ephrem calls on You to be merciful to his "children"—the people in his city of Nisibis—by asking You to remember Your own
childhood and have mercy on those who resemble it. These child-
hoods are intertwined: the childhood of Your eternal youthfulness,
the childhood of Your life as the Christ, the childhood You call
us to, and the children who witness to that childhood. Children

image to us both Your childhood of eternal youthfulness and the childhood to which we are called, and Your childhood as Christ links the image with the imaged, the natural childhood of children with the spiritual childhood to which we are called and in which we find You, the eternally young.

Come to us, O Lord, in the little children around us. Come to us in those who demand our attention, who want more than we feel we can give. Come to us in the ones who wake us in the night and see us as braver and stronger than we believe ourselves to be. Come to us in those who seem never to tire of our games and tricks, in those whose playfulness seems boundless and mysterious. Come to us in those who teach us to love, play, and wait more than we imagined we ever would. Come to us in those who arrived in our lives as strangers and are now becoming our friends.

To learn to love a stranger like my daughter once was to find You in a stranger. Through my little stranger, I learn better to love a stranger like You. And I hope my love and my life prepare my own friend-in-the-making to love strangers and to receive their love.

This love by which strangers become friends stands behind the relationship of the material and immaterial, the fleshly and the spiritual, Creator and creation. We become Your friends because You became what was strange to divinity that we might see You and know You better. And in this friendship, You the Creator invite us into a new kinship, one that makes us like You, the eternal Child. In baptism, You gave me the font of Your eternal youth, but the time is late, Lord, and I have grown old. Renew me in Your youth once again, God. Again!

CHAPTER 13

Creation

A body by its weight tends to move towards its proper place.
Once they are in their ordered position, they are at rest . . .

My weight is my love.

The creation story of Genesis 1 heaps on vivid images, one after another—wind sweeping over the dark deep, waters gathering and uncovering dry lands, seas swarming with fish and sea monsters—before ending with a creature who is named as an image: humankind, in the image of God You created them, male and female You created them. You bless them, consecrate all green vegetation to their needs, and declare this creation good—no, on this day You declare Your creation *very* good. In some ways, the chapter ending is fitting and beautiful, the culmination of all the prior moments of creation, as this last creation points back to You the Creator. In other ways, it is strange, for the chapter break divides the days of creation. The image-bearers appear on day six, not day seven. Genesis 1 ends before creation is quite finished, and chapter 2 opens on the seventh day, when You hallow Your creation, and rest. That is how the work of creation ends: with rest.

The creation narrative of Genesis 1 has been differently interpreted throughout the tradition. It has been construed as a poem for Your people in exile to remember who You are, a rival to scientific accounts of the universe's origins, and a justification for ignoring human damage to the world. In his own rendition, Augustine reads Genesis 1 as a story about the Church. The dry land is the faithful, restrained from the sea of desires and thirsty for You. The fish and the whales are the sacraments of initiation and miraculous wonders that convert an unbelieving and uncatechized people. The statement that humankind images You instructs humans to be renewed in their minds, an injunction Augustine returns to throughout the *Confessions*. In these ways, Augustine interprets the story of creation by an allegory of re-creation, a move particularly powerful because, for him, allegory speaks not just to the text but to the world. The text is not freighted with meaning differently than the world. Lambs in texts signify Christ because all lambs do. And the dry land of Genesis 1 signifies thirst for You because all dry land signifies such thirst.

The book that begins with the claim that our hearts are restless until they rest in You arrives, finally, in the rest of creation. Augustine writes that in the Sabbath of eternal life, You will rest in us and through us as now You work in us and through us. You who never stops working, who never ceases from doing good, are also the perfect rest. You are the Sabbath You invite us into, the Sabbath of eternal life, in which we as creation enter a new intimacy with You as Creator.

Praising You as the God who continually works and perpetually rests, Augustine asks: How can a human mind hope to understand this? He answers, "Only you can be asked, only you can be begged, only on your door can we knock. Yes indeed, that is how it is received, how it is found, how the door is opened." His contemplation of Genesis 1 leads him to this image of opening, in which the readers are invited to approach a threshold of greater understanding and divine presence. We reach the threshold by the desire that makes us not just ask, but knock and beg. By love we draw near Love. By love our door opens.

Like many readers, Augustine spends more time on the elegant, structured account of Genesis 1 than the more meandering story of creation that takes up most of Genesis 2. But over the years, I have pressed my students to read Genesis 1 and 2 together, prodding them to compare the two creation accounts and to wonder over their discrepancies. Why would the people of God preserve over the centuries, I ask them, these two contradictory accounts of creation, with their obviously divergent chronologies? What work are these stories supposed to do? By the time we take up this puzzle, we have spent a couple of weeks thinking theologically about creation, and so the students are prepared to reflect deeply on these Scriptural accounts. We work through Genesis 1, with its lovely order, the first three days of creating forms reflected in the second three days of filling those very forms: the sun, stars, and moon of day 4 filling the light and darkness of day 1; the birds and fish of day 5 filling the skies and waters of day 2; the land animals of day 6 filling the dry lands of day 3. After we admire this structure, I ask the class where You appear in the story. Students do not need to consult their texts to answer. They know: You appear only as a voice from beyond. In Genesis 1, You are a God remote from the world, a God of order and beauty and transcendence. But what about the second creation account? In Genesis 2, You are down in the garden, scooping up dust and breathing life into it. You are a God who is in the world, unafraid of being soiled by it. You appear in our very dirt. Why these different pictures of You? We decide together that the juxtaposition of the two creation accounts expresses both Your beyondness and presence to creation. This juxtaposition offers poetically what the class has up to that point been learning with large theological abstractions like "non-contrastive transcendence." Genesis 1 and 2 together communicate a God who is both beyond the highest heavens and present to the smallest among us, the way You are here but You cannot be contained by here—an idea that runs throughout the *Confessions*, from the opening words to the final book.

As committed as he is to the uncontainability of God, Augustine allegorizes only the lofty Genesis 1 picture of God in Book XIII of the *Confessions*. How might including Genesis 2, where God is present in something as small and lowly as dirt, thicken his account of creation as re-creation? What if, even as the creation story can point to something as grand as Your church, it can also point to something as small as life coming to be in a pregnant body? This, after all, is where I keep finding You, in the life You have given me to love. The daughter who came to me through pregnancy and labor has born in me a new love, and through the work of learning to be faithful to that love, I find Your rest.

What if I return to the creation stories of Genesis 1 and 2 with my daughter's life in my mind? It is easy to see affinities with pregnancy in them. In the beginning of the creating of the child, the womb was dark and void, and the divine breath moved over the waters of the deep. The waters bring forth life, and the human is in Your image, and is given the command to do as was done in generating her own womb-dwelling: to be fruitful and multiply. And as You worked out Your creation with something as insignificant, even despised, as dirt, so can I see You working out Your creation through a substance even more disdained, the blood of a woman's body. I can see my daughter as the literal bone of my bone, flesh of my flesh, the creature given life from my very body; her genesis can speak to the genesis of the world, and the world's genesis to hers.

Gregory of Nyssa, like many church fathers and Greek philosophers, describes humanity as a *microcosmos*. He gives the word to his sister Macrina, who proclaims humanity a *microcosmos* in one of Gregory's dialogues on the nature of humanity, death, and resurrection. He is thinking particularly of the way the material and spiritual dimensions of the person, the body and the soul, mirror the visible and invisible elements of the world. What can be found in the universe can be found in miniature in the human, which gives the human an important place in the universe. She stands between the purely spiritual nature of angels and the purely material nature of beasts, binding them into a cosmic whole.

There is an analogy here. As the human body is a *microcosmos*, the pregnant woman's body is a microgenesis. Readings of Your incarnation in Mary's body often suggest this, even if they do not claim it outright. Mary's body is presented as a new creation. Mary's words "let it be done to me" (*fiat mihi* in the longtime language of the Church) echo Your words at creation "let there be light" (*fiat lux*). The Spirit hovering over the waters of the deep, formless and empty, hovers over the waters of Mary's womb, once again bringing life into a dark void. The incarnation is a new creation, and theologians and artists have over the centuries dramatized its echoes of and parallels to the first creation. The first creation gave us Adam; the second, the new Adam, Christ. From the body of a woman, the Spirit makes a new creation.

The *fiat mihi* of the second creation is so personal, so intimate, so quiet compared to the *fiat lux* of the first. At one level, it seems much less majestic. With the *fiat lux*, light is created that makes physical sight possible. In the *fiat mihi*, a babe enters Mary's womb, invisibly. The world looks absolutely the same, and yet the world has entirely changed. Can I imagine anything more transcendent? Humanity has been re-created, reborn by Mary's words. You enter a relationship with humanity even more intimate than that of Creator and creature; You open the creature so she can enter more deeply into the divine life. In this intensely personal moment, You become present to us in a new way.

I am sitting next to my daughter now and thinking of all the ways she has become present to me since and even prior to her own birth, and the ways I have learned to be present to her. We are both reading and writing, each of us immersed in our work of the moment. Every once in a while she looks up at me and smiles, and sometimes we share something we have just read. She giggles and relays a witticism from Hermione Granger. I pause to ask her what she thinks about Augustine's Eucharistic fish. She finds them "disgusting" and is very glad the Eucharist she eats is bread, not meat. I think of George Herbert's poem describing the Eucharist precisely as meat and decide not to tell my passionate vegetarian about it just yet. For this moment, I feel my work drained of the anxiety that sometimes washes over it. My daughter's life tempts me to new forms of domination, but it also helps me learn to resist domination and practice fidelity to the way of love. In Augustine's language, she helps me find the weight of my love. Her life opens me to You in a new way so that by her life, I see You better, creation better, and Mary better.

In the Annunciation, Mary's body becomes pregnant with You who are Life itself. A human home for divine presence, she becomes the first church. She is sometimes called a model or type of the Church, the one who is the Church *en nuce* and who reveals something about the Church's own motherhood. The Church, in some theological documents, is encouraged to strive after the blemishless existence already attained by Mary.

And Mary and the Church both, like You, labor for the world. Mary's labor figures, reveals, and clarifies the Church's own labor. The Church, like Mary, labors to bear divine presence into the world. The Church, like Mary, participates in Your new creation and hearkens to Your first. In the figure of Mary, creation, church, and pregnancy all entwine as images of one another. A pregnant woman's body, the Church expectant, and You, the womb of creation, all come together in the image of pregnancy. What if I followed Augustine's principle of reading the world allegorically, as if, like Scriptures, it, too, is saturated with divine presence? What would I find in my own labor with my daughter?

I think back to the tub, the water, the pain, the gift, the blood—and read them together with the images of Scripture. Following Mary, following You who mothers us to life, the expectant Mother-Church labors for us all to be reborn as little christs, her waters of parturition baptizing us, the body and blood she gives nourishing us. She struggles to bring us to life and light. With all creation, the Mother-Church groans in her birth pains, waiting for the arrival of Christ that will end her labor. She wants, I remember, to open and receive a new presence. Imitating and sustained by Your own motherhood, she labors on, anticipating in hope the eternal rest of new creation crowning.

ACKNOWLEDGMENTS

My first expression of gratitude goes to the students of my Introduction to Theology classes over the years. I'm thankful to them for wondering with me about Augustine's *Confessions*, for letting it speak to them, and for being willing to speak back to it. I hope you all find your way to love that grows ever stronger and deeper and to work sustained by a heart at rest.

If the project began in conversations with students, it was nurtured by myriad others. Emily-Jane Cohen believed in this quirky project and supported it until her last day at Stanford University Press. I know I am not the only author who will miss her immensely competent presence there. I am grateful to her and to Kate Wahl and Faith Wilson Stein for shepherding the project through SUP.

Many colleagues at Baylor have supported me throughout writing and in various ways, especially Brooke Blevins, Jamie van Eyck Beceiro, Candi Cann, Elise Edwards, Barry Harvey, Lynn Hinojosa, Victor Hinojosa, Alan Jacobs, Rob Miner, Paul Martens, Kristen Pond, among others. Cat Jonathan Tran has promoted the project, and Baylor as an institution has supported it directly. On that last front, I wish to give an especial thanks to Bill Bellinger, Kim Kellison, and Truell Hyde for the financial backing they helped secure. Their support generated a better book and a pleasanter writing process, not least because it enabled me to work with Lauren Winner. Lauren has helped me develop the ear, eye, and hand to write for different audiences. I found her instincts invariably right, and she was fun to work with as well.

When the manuscript was a very rough first draft, Greg Lee read every word of it and offered his expertise as a reader and a scholar of Augustine. I owe him a debt for both his encouragement and his advice, which he gave in a spirit of friendship and good humor, despite being in an extremely busy period of his own life. Other colleagues have supported the project as well, including Sheryl Overmyer, Michelle Harrington, and Sean Larsen.

Throughout the writing process, I presented portions of this manuscript at the American Academy of Religion, the Society for the Study of Theology, and a St Andrews Monday night bible study. At each venue, I was surprised by its openhearted reception and am grateful to those audiences, particularly the people who shared their own stories with me afterwards.

Other friends, both scholars and otherwise, have listened to the project, asked about it, and expressed enthusiasm for it, buoying me with a feeling of community throughout my writing. Chief among these supportive friends have been my extended family, for which I am exceedingly fortunate. In a book about motherhood, I want to recognize especially my own mother and also my father, whose sacrifices, gifts, and journey have become more vivid to me since becoming a parent myself.

Closer to the end of the project, Maggi Jones and Thomas Breedlove assisted by copyediting it. Both of them offered sharp-eyed assessments that improved the manuscript, and I am grateful to them. Throughout the drafting, revising, and editing processes,

Courtney Haworth spent many hours delighting my children, and I learned a great deal from Kyndall Rothaus as well.

Of course, the ones I owe the most appear in the book itself. For though, at one level, the project began with my students, at another, it began, followed, and ended in life with my family. I am grateful to my husband, Matthew, who not only supported me in his usual ways of discussing, reading, and editing my work, but also in the extraordinary way of allowing me to expose our life together, even some of its painful aspects. His presence in my life is greater than the reader can discern from the story, but Matthew's love has seen me through both the writing of this book and the journey it chronicles.

And then there are my daughters—Chora, Edith, and Simone. You girls birthed me into motherhood and call me daily into a deeper, freer, more difficult love. You are diversely beautiful and astonishingly strong, each of you a gift I could never have anticipated. This book—how could it be any other way?—is for you.

AUTHOR'S NOTE

While the story narrated here is based on my experiences as a mother, I have modified some of the events in my telling of them. I have three daughters, not just one, and I have pulled episodes from the lives of all of them into this story. In some episodes, siblings played a crucial role, and so I have found ways of working around their absence in the book while maintaining the fidelity to my memory in the best way I could.

One more important change: All the names have been altered to protect people's privacy.

NOTES

PREFACE

Augustine writes: Augustine, *Confessions*, trans. Henry Chadwick (New York: Oxford University Press, 1990), I.6.9, p. 7. **The first mention**: John 3:1–16 (New Revised Standard Version). **Augustine describes this woman**: Augustine, *Confessions*, VI.15.25, p. 109.

CHAPTER 1

How shall I call upon my God: Augustine, *Confessions*, I.2.3, p. 4. **I think we all want to know**: Fran Bagenal, speaking on *Morning Edition*, NPR, July 3, 2016, audio, http://www.npr.org/templates/transcript/transcript. php?storyId=482534266. **Whatever is done for the least of these**: Matthew 25:31–46 (NRSV). **I was the Christ who first**: John Chrysostom makes this point in the 45th homily on the Gospel of Matthew. See John Chrysostom, "Homily 45 on Matthew," trans. George Prevost and revised by M.B. Riddle, *Nicene and Post-Nicene Fathers, First Series*, Vol. 10, eds. Philip Schaff and Henry Wace (Buffalo, NY: Christian Literature Publishing Co., 1890), revised and edited for New Advent website by Kevin Knight, http://www.newadvent.org/fathers/200145.htm. **One study reports**: Rina J. Kara, Paola Bolli, Ioannis Karakikes, Iwao Matsunaga, Joseph Tripodi, Omar Tanweer, Perry Altman, Neil S. Shachter, Austin Nakano, Vesna Najfeld, and Hina W. Chaudhry, "Fetal Cells Traffic to Injured Maternal Myocardium and Undergo Cardiac Differentiation," *Circulation Research* 110.1 (January 6, 2012): 82–93, http://circres.ahajournals.org/content/110/1/82. **Margaret Mead once wrote**:

Margaret Mead, *Male and Female: A Study of the Sexes in a Changing World* (New York: New American Library, 1959), 284. Quoted in Valerie Saiving Goldstein, "The Human Situation: A Feminine View," *Journal of Religion* 40.2 (April 1960): 100–12. **Augustine describes his infant self:** Augustine, *Confessions*, I.7.11, p. 9. **Augustine observed the desire:** Ibid. **Hrdy casts the story:** Sarah Blaffer Hrdy, *Mothers and Others: The Evolutionary Origins of Mutual Understanding* (Cambridge, MA: Belknap, 2011), 40. **The first mission of a mammal baby:** Ibid., 41. **Hrdy thinks of a mother dog:** Ibid., 39. **Once a mother and child have suckled:** Ibid., 72. **For the good which came to me:** Augustine, *Confessions*, I.6.7, p. 6. **Sara Ruddick tells a story:** Sara Ruddick, *Maternal Thinking: Toward a Politics of Peace* (Boston: Beacon Press, 1989), 65–7.

CHAPTER 2

You gathered me together: Augustine, *Confessions*, II.1.1, p. 24. **In their perverted way:** Ibid., II.6.14, p. 32. **Jesus don't you see:** Luke 10:41–2 (NRSV). **Telling the tale to a novice:** I heard this story in a class on Cappadocian Theology taught in fall 2000 at Harvard Divinity School by Dr. Nicholas Constas, now Father Maximos Constas. **Right from the first days of life:** Hrdy, *Mothers and Others*, 7. **an experiment in the 1970s:** Ibid., 47–50. The experiment Hrdy discusses was conducted by Andrew Meltzoff and Keith Moore. **In this second experiment:** Ibid., 56–60. The second experiment was conducted by Tetsuro Matsuzawa and Masako Myowa. **A human child is born eager:** Ibid., 23. **The rate of infants:** "Sudden Unexpected Infant Death Syndrome and Sudden Infant Death Syndrome," Center for Disease Control, last modified June 28, 2018, https://www.cdc.gov/sids/data.htm. **Emmelia joked:** Gregory of Nyssa makes this joke in his hagiography of his sister, *The Life of Macrina.* **her advice seemed to him "womanish":** Augustine, *Confessions*, II.3.7, p. 27. *I must decrease:* John 3:30 (NRSV). **not made for children:** Maria Montessori, *The Child in the Church*, ed. E.M. Standing (Chantilly, VA: The Madonna and Child Atrium, 1965), 7.

CHAPTER 3

Why is it that a person: Augustine, *Confessions*, III.2.2, p. 36. **There was love between him and the child:** George Eliot, *Silas Marner* (New York: Oxford, 2017), 118. **eyes more demanding:** Roger Ebert, "Review:

Tsotsi," March 9, 2006, http://www.rogerebert.com/reviews/tsotsi-2006. **She would have been the perfect mom**: Quoted in Michelle Dean, "Dee Dee Wanted Her Daughter To Be Sick, Gypsy Wanted Her Mom To Be Murdered," *BuzzFeed News*, August 18, 2016, https://www.buzzfeed.com/michelledean/dee-dee-wanted-her-daughter-to-be-sick-gypsy-wanted-her-mom?utm_term=.nlrnDGZGMm#.onJPgwowa2. **I once had a teacher**: The teacher is Elaine Scarry, who writes of lateral regard in *On Beauty and Being Just* (Princeton, NJ: Princeton University Press, 2001). **The book changed my feelings**: Augustine, *Confessions*, III.4.7, p. 39. **Lord, he whom you love**: John 11:3 (NRSV). **[E]ven now I know that God**: John 11:22 (NRSV). **is greatly disturbed**: John 11:33 (NRSV). **Has any one of us wept**: Pope Francis, homily during visit to Lampedusa, July 8, 2013, https://w2.vatican.va/content/francesco/en/homilies/2013/documents/papa-francesco_20130708_omelia-lampedusa.html. **You heard her**: Augustine, *Confessions*, III.11.19, p. 49. **Go away from me**: Ibid., III.12.21, p. 51. **as if they sounded from heaven**: Ibid.

CHAPTER 4

What madness not to understand: Augustine, *Confessions*, IV.7.12, p. 59. **The condition of black life**: Claudia Rankine, "'The Condition of Black Life Is One of Mourning,'" *New York Times Magazine*, June 22, 2015, https://www.nytimes.com/2015/06/22/magazine/the-condition-of-black-life-is-one-of-mourning.html. **White children**: James Baldwin, *No Name in the Street* (New York: Dial Press, 1972; New York: Vintage Paperback, 2000), 128. My thanks to Sean Larsen for his incisive readings of Baldwin. **[Y]ou can only be destroyed**: James Baldwin, *The Fire Next Time* (New York: Dial Press, 1963; New York: Vintage Paperback, 1993), 4. In Baldwin's original, he used the full word for n——r. **He mentions films**: Ta-Nehisi Coates, *Between the World and Me* (New York: Spiegel & Grau, 2015), 32. **Delores Williams challenged**: Delores Williams, *Sisters in the Wilderness: The Challenge of Womanist God-Talk* (Maryknoll, NY: Orbis Books, 1993). See also Jacquelyn Grant, *White Women's Christ and Black Women's Jesus: Feminist Christology and Womanist Response* (Atlanta, GA: Scholars Press, 1989). **How stupid is man**: Augustine, *Confessions*, IV.7.12, p. 59. **What madness**: Ibid. **Let the people see what I see**: Rankine, "'The Condition of Black Life Is One of Mourning.'"

CHAPTER 5

Where was I when I was seeking: Augustine, *Confessions*, V.2.2, p. 81.
Reading Rachel Cusk: Rachel Cusk, *A Life's Work: On Becoming a Mother*
(New York: Picador, 2001), 33. **I am surprised to discover**: Ibid., 56.
They are nested baskets of conversion stories: E. Ann Matter makes a
similar point. See "Conversion(s) in the *Confessiones*," in *Collectanea Augustinanana*, eds. Joseph Schnaubelt and Frederick van Fleteren (Leuven:
Leuven University Press, 1990), 25. **Not in riots and drunken parties**:
Romans 13:13–14, as quoted in Augustine, *Confessions*, VIII.7.29, p. 153.
at once: Augustine, *Confessions*, VIII.7.29, p. 153. **It is peaceful. I am
grateful**: Allia A. Matta, "Revolving Doors: Mother-Woman Rhythms
in Academic Spaces," in *Mothers in Academia*, eds. Maria Castañeda and
Kirsten Isgro (New York: Columbia University Press, 2013), 147. **the
signature of childhood**: Alison Gopnik, *The Philosophical Baby: What
Children's Minds Tell Us About Truth, Love and the Meaning of Life* (New
York: Farrar, Straus and Giroux, 2009), 14. Quoted in Robert Bellah,
Religion in Human Evolution: From the Paleolithic to the Axial Age (Cambridge, MA: Belknap, 2011), 89. **David is willing to be silly**: II Samuel
6:14 (NRSV). **It is how you create a symbolic world**: It was an insight
of Johan Huizinga in *Homo Ludens* that the opposite of play is not seriousness, but work. Play can be very serious. Freud knew the seriousness
of play, too. He wrote, "Might we not say that every child at play behaves
like a creative writer, in that he creates a world of his own, or, rather, rearranges the things of his world in a new way which pleases him?" Freud,
"Creative Writers and Day-Dreaming," *The Freud Reader*, ed. Peter Gay
(New York: Norton, 1999), 437. **Through play we learn to be human**:
Play is the central turning point in the development of the human in
Robert Bellah's masterful last work, *Religion in Human Evolution*. He
makes the connection between play and religion on page 110. **The child,
when it plays**: Romano Guardini, *The Spirit of the Liturgy*, trans. Ada
Lane (New York: Sheed & Ward, 1935; Chicago: Biretta Books, 2014),
42. **the rediscovering within us**: Joseph Ratzinger, *Spirit of the Liturgy*,
trans. John Saward (San Francisco: Ignatius Press, 2000), 140. **A woman
retains**: Jia Tolentino, "When Women Signify Too Much," *New Yorker*,
October 5, 2016, http://www.newyorker.com/culture/jia-tolentino/
when-women-signify-too-much. **How do you know what you want**:

Jaclyn Friedman, "I'm a sexual consent educator. Here's what's missing in the Aziz Ansari conversation," *Vox*, January 19, 2018, https://www. vox.com/first-person/2018/1/19/16907246/sexual-consent-educator-aziz-ansari. **enculturated to be uncomfortable**: Lili Loofbourow, "The Female Price of Male Pleasure," *The Week*, January 25, 2018, http:// theweek.com/articles/749978/female-price-male-pleasure. **Your play prepares you to be an adult**: Rowan Williams makes this point in his chapter on childhood in *Lost Icons: Reflections on Cultural Bereavement* (Edinburgh: T & T Clark, 2000). **an island without clocks**: Adrienne Rich describes being in just such a situation for one summer as one of her most positive experiences of motherhood. *Of Woman Born: Motherhood as Experience and Institution* (New York: W.W. Norton, 1976).

CHAPTER 6

As soon as he saw blood: Augustine, *Confessions*, VI.8.13, p. 101. **sorrowful and agitated**: Matthew 26:37 (NRSV). **deeply grieved**: Matthew 26:39 (NRSV). **Friend, do what you are here to do**: Matthew 26:50 (NRSV). **an absorbent self**: Though this phase is commonly called "the absorbent mind" in Montessori's work, and her most famous book is so titled, Montessori began to shift toward the end of her life to "the absorbent self," which reflected the rich sensorial life of the child. As she said in one of the talks collected in *The Absorbent Mind*, "The child *absorbs* impressions not with his mind but with life itself." Maria Montessori, *The Absorbent Mind*, trans. John Chattin-McNichols (New York: Henry Holt, 1995), 24. **The twin temptations for coming of age**: Stanley Cavell, "A Cover Letter to Molière's *Misanthrope*," in *Themes Out of School: Effects and Causes* (San Francisco: North Point Press, 1984), 97–105.

CHAPTER 7

What torments my heart suffered: Augustine, *Confessions*, VII.7.11, p. 120. **Woman, what concern**: John 2:4 (NRSV). **the first of his signs**: John 2:11 (NRSV). **Everyone serves the good wine first**: John 2:10 (NRSV). **Hail, King of the Jews**: Versions of these taunts can be found in multiple gospels. See Matthew 27:27–31, 39–44; Mark 15:16–20, 29–32; Luke 23:35–39; and John 19:3 (NRSV). **as a person dead**: Augustine, *Confessions*, VI.1.1, p. 90. **[S]he did not leap for joy**: Ibid. **daily and tearfully prayed**: Ibid. **What Montessori wants**: Themes of freedom, independence, and peace run throughout Maria Montessori's corpus, including in works like *The Secret of Childhood, The Child, Society, and the World, The Absorbent Mind,* and *Education and Peace.*

CHAPTER 8

But my madness with myself: Augustine, VIII.8.19, p. 146. **Then you shall call:** Isaiah 58:9 (NRSV). **Assuming that he was:** Luke 2:44–56 (NRSV). **Child, why have you:** Luke 2:47 (NRSV). **Mary's betrothed:** Luke 1:27 (NRSV). **one whose lineage:** Luke 2:4; 3:23 (NRSV). **companion of Mary:** Luke 2:16 (NRSV). **when he found out:** Matthew 1:18–25. **Why were you searching:** Luke 2:49 (NRSV). **the son (as was thought) of Joseph:** Luke 3:23 (NRSV). **Is not this Joseph's son?** : Luke 4:22 (NRSV). **Go in peace:** I Samuel 1:17 (NRSV). **leaves him there:** I Samuel 1:28 (NRSV). **The horse and the rider:** Exodus 15:21 (NRSV). **God has scattered:** Luke 1:52–3 (NRSV). **Here I am:** Genesis 22:1 (NRSV). **Abraham answers:** Genesis 22:7 (NRSV). **a very poignant moment:** Jonathan Safran Foer, "Jonathan Safran Foer on Marriage, Religion and Universal Balances," interview by Terry Gross, *Fresh Air*, NPR, November 10, 2016, rebroadcast July 7, 2017, http://www.npr.org/2017/07/07/535969620/jonathan-safran-foer-on-marriage-religion-and-universal-balances. **God himself will provide:** Genesis 22:8 (NRSV). **going to pieces:** Maggie Nelson, *The Argonauts* (Minneapolis, MN: Graywolf Press, 2015), 84. **But where through so many years:** Augustine, *Confessions,* IX.1.1, p. 155. **in form and raiment:** Gregory of Nyssa, *The Life of Macrina,* 120. **There life is the wisdom:** Augustine, *Confessions,* IX.10.24, p. 171. **Make the leap:** Ibid., VIII.11.27, p. 151.

CHAPTER 9

In the place: Augustine, *Confessions,* IX.4.10, p. 162. The full section after the colon reads "there you began to be my delight, and you gave 'gladness is my heart'" (Ps. 4:7). **the injunction in Leviticus:** Leviticus 12:8. **prophetic words:** Luke 2:34–5 (NRSV). **[T]he Presentation is portrayed:** Father Maximos Constas, *The Art of Seeing: Paradox and Perception in Orthodox Iconography* (Brookline, MA: Holy Cross Orthodox Press, 2014), 103–4. **Come to me:** Paul Evdokimov, *The Art of the Icon: A Theology of Beauty,* trans. Father Steven Bigham (Redondo Beach, CA: Oakwood Press, 1972), 325. **saying to Adam:** Ibid., 323.

CHAPTER 10

This power of memory: Augustine, *Confessions*, X.8.15, p. 187. **he was not with You**: Ibid., X.27.38, p. 201. **a huge cavern**: Ibid., X.8.13, p. 186. **coerced into confessing a murder**: Rachel Aviv, "Remembering the Murder You Didn't Commit," *New Yorker*, June 19, 2017, http://www.newyorker.com/magazine/2017/06/19/remembering-the-murder-you-didnt-commit. **This power of memory**: Augustine, *Confessions*, X.8.15, p. 187. **According to legend**: This version of the story is told in the popular medieval collection of saint's lives, *The Golden Legend* by Jacobus de Voragine. For a complete English edition see Jacobus de Voragine, *The Golden Legend: Readings on the Saints*, trans. William Granger Ryan (Princeton, NJ: Princeton University Press, 2012). **In one account**: Socrates Scholasticus, *Ecclesiastical History*, trans. A. C. Zenos, *Nicene and Post-Nicene Fathers, Second Series*, Vol. 2, eds. Philip Schaff and Henry Wace (Buffalo, NY: Christian Literature Publishing Co., 1890), revised and edited for New Advent website by Kevin Knight, http://www.newadvent.org/fathers/26017.htm, Book VII, Chapter 15. **Another tells a similar story**: Bishop John of Nikiu, *Chronicle* (London: Williams & Norgate, 1916), 84.102, http://www.tertullian.org/fathers/nikiu2_chronicle.htm. **See how widely I have ranged**: Augustine, *Confessions*, X.24.35, p. 200.

CHAPTER 11

It is not in time: Augustine, *Confessions*, XI.13.16, p. 230. **Augustine mused once**: Augustine addresses our ages and other questions about the resurrection in *City of God*, trans. Henry Bettenson (London and New York: Penguin Classics, 2003), Book 22, pp. 1022–91. **I think of Ted Hughes's poem**: I discovered this poem in an essay by Cora Diamond, "The Difficulty of Reality and the Difficulty of Philosophy," *Partial Answers: Journal of Literature and the History of Ideas* 1:2 (June 2003): 1–26. **His last stanza**: Ted Hughes, "Six Young Men," *The Hawk in the Rain* (London: Faber and Faber, 1957), 54–5. **categorical superiority of icons**: Evdokimov makes this point about remembrance and presence throughout his book *Art of the Icon*, but especially in pages 178–80. **picture theorist Hans Belting**: Hans Belting, *An Anthropology of Images: Picture, Medium, Body*, trans. Thomas Dunlap (Princeton, NJ: Princeton University Press, 2014). **As Augustine asks**: Augustine,

Confessions, XI.8.15, p. 229. **You have made time itself**: Ibid. **Gregory raises but does not resolve**: Gregory of Nyssa engages in this exercising of wondering about our spiritual bodies through his characters Gregory and Macrina toward the end of *On the Soul and the Resurrection*. **created all times**: Augustine, *Confessions*, XI.8.16, p. 230. **Your 'years'**: Ibid. **Thus, my boyhood**: Ibid., XI.18.23, p. 234. **that shoulders Augustine out of the ordinary**: The phrase is from Diamond, "The Difficulty of Reality and the Difficulty of Philosophy." **Who can deny**: Augustine, *Confessions*, XI.28.37, p. 243. **With Augustine**: Ibid., XI.25.32, p. 239.

CHAPTER 12

You were, the rest was nothing: Augustine, *Confessions*, XII.7.7, p. 249. **derived from you**: Ibid., XII.15.21, p. 256. **the mystery of Your embodiment**: Maximus the Confessor, "Ambiguum 7," translated and quoted in Paul Blowers, *Maximus the Confessor: Jesus Christ and the Transfiguration of the World* (Oxford: Oxford University Press, 2016), 73. **from Gregory of Nazianzus**: Quoted in Blowers, *Maximus the Confessor*, 86. I have modified Paul Blowers's translation of Gregory of Nazianzus's poem slightly. **Chesterton imagines**: G. K. Chesterton, *Orthodoxy* (New York: John Lane Company, 1909; Louisville, KY: GLH Publishing, 2016), 57. **beautiful hymns**: Ephrem the Syrian, "Nisibene Hymns: Hymn 4," trans. J. T. Sarsfield Stopford, *Nicene and Post-Nicene Fathers, Second Series*, Vol. 13, eds. Philip Schaff and Henry Wace (Buffalo, NY: Christian Literature Publishing Co., 1890), revised and edited for New Advent website by Kevin Knight, http://www.newadvent.org/fathers/3702b.htm.

CHAPTER 13

A body by its weight: Augustine, *Confessions*, XIII.9.10, p. 278. The entire passage reads, "A body by its weight tends to move towards its proper place. The weight's movement is not necessarily downwards, but to its appropriate position: fire tends to move upwards, a stone downwards. They are acted on by their respective weights; they seek their own place. Oil poured under water is drawn up to the surface on top of the water. Water poured on top of oil sinks below the oil. They are acted on by their respective densities, they seek their own place. Things which are not in their intended position are restless. Once they are in their ordered position, they are at rest. My weight is my love." **In his own rendition**:

Ibid., XIII.17.20, p. 284. **The fish and the whales**: Ibid., XIII.27.42, p. 299. **Sabbath of eternal life**: Ibid., XIII.37.52, p. 304. **Only you can be asked**: Ibid., XIII.37.53, p. 305. **a *microcosmos***: This analogy is found in Gregory of Nyssa, *On the Soul and the Resurrection.*

ENCOUNTERING TRADITIONS